Th. Jefferson

Embrace the past

JAYNE D'ALESSANDRO-COX

Th. Jefferson

FROM BOY TO MAN

Time Period 1743-1774

"Adore God. Reverence and cherish your parents.
Love your neighbor as yourself, and your country
more than yourself. Be just. Be true. Murmur not
at the ways of Providence." [1]

TATE PUBLISHING
AND ENTERPRISES, LLC

Thomas Jefferson - From Boy to Man
Second Edition
Copyright © 2015 by Jayne D'Alessandro-Cox. All rights reserved.

The opinions expressed by the author are not necessarily those of Tate Publishing, LLC.

Published by Tate Publishing & Enterprises, LLC
127 E. Trade Center Terrace | Mustang, Oklahoma 73064 USA
1.888.361.9473 | www.tatepublishing.com

Tate Publishing is committed to excellence in the publishing industry. The company reflects the philosophy established by the founders, based on Psalm 68:11,
"The Lord gave the word and great was the company of those who published it."

Book design copyright © 2015 by Tate Publishing, LLC. All rights reserved.
Cover design by Jan Sunday Quilaquil
Interior design by Deborah Toling

Published in the United States of America

ISBN: 978-1-62746-258-7
1. History / United States / Colonial Period (1600-1775)
2. Biography & Autobiography / Historical
15.07.29

Dedication

I dedicate this book to the memory of Rob Coles, a Gentleman in the finest tradition of the University, as well as to his family. It was an honor and a pleasure to research and document the first thirty-one years of his fascinating, charismatic and very likeable ancestor... Thomas Jefferson.

I also dedicate this book to the enslaved African-Americans and indentured servants who were instrumental in building our great nation. We must remember *their* story.

Acknowledgments

A special thank you is extended to:

The Thomas Jefferson Foundation, Charlottesville, Virginia

The Jefferson Library at Monticello, Charlottesville, Virginia

The Colonial Williamsburg Foundation, Williamsburg, Virginia

The College of William & Mary, Williamsburg, Virginia

The John D. Rockefeller, Jr. Library, Williamsburg, Virginia

The Earl Gregg Swem Library, Williamsburg, Virginia

The Bruton Heights School, Williamsburg, Virginia

The Muscarelle Museum of Art at the College of William & Mary in Virginia

I wish to acknowledge the following people who contributed generously to this book, and were instrumental throughout the many months of research. I greatly appreciate your professionalism, incredible attention to detail, and willingness to assist with all and any requested information promptly and thoroughly. It was an honor and a privilege to correspond with you.

Dr. Taylor Stoermer, Historian, John D. Rockefeller, Jr. Library, Colonial Williamsburg Foundation

Marianne Martin, Visual Resources Librarian, John D. Rockefeller, Jr. Library, Colonial Williamsburg Foundation

Juleigh Muirhead Clark, Public Services Librarian, John D. Rockefeller, Jr. Library, Colonial Williamsburg Foundation

Allison Heinbaugh, Reference Librarian, John D. Rockefeller Library, Colonial Williamsburg Foundation

Melissa Parris, Head of Collections and Exhibitions Management, The Muscarelle Museum of Art, The College of William & Mary

Tom Austin, Photo Services Manager, John D. Rockefeller, Jr. Library, Colonial Williamsburg Foundation

George Yetter, Associate Curator of Architectural Collections, John D. Rockefeller, Jr. Library, Colonial Williamsburg Foundation

Alan Zoellner, English Subject and Government Information Librarian, The Earl Gregg Swem Library, College of Williams & Mary

Benjamin Bromley, Public Services Archivist, Earl Gregg Swem Library, College of William & Mary

Paul Aron, Director of Publications, Colonial Williamsburg Foundation

Barbara Temple Lombardi, Photographer/Digital Technician, Colonial Williamsburg Foundation

Rachel E. Merkley, Wythe House Site Supervisor, Department of Historic Sites Interpretation, Colonial Williamsburg Foundation

Anne Conkling, Volunteer Coordinator and Supervisor, The Bruton Parish Church, Colonial Williamsburg

Historical Interpreters, Colonial Williamsburg Foundation

Bill Barker, Colonial Williamsburg Nation Builder, as Thomas Jefferson

Savannah Williams as Rebecca Burwell Ambler

Annalise Weindel as Martha Jefferson

Joseph Ziarko as Edmund Randolph

Chris Hull as George Wythe and Peyton Randolph

Actor Alex Morse at the Apollo Room, Raleigh Tavern

Gertrude A. Ivory, Associate Superintendent of Curriculum & Instruction, Charlottesville City Schools, Charlottesville, Virginia

Anne Evans, Coordinator of Social Studies, Charlottesville City Schools, Charlottesville, Virginia

Rob Coles, 5th great-grandson of Thomas Jefferson, Charlottesville, Virignia

Robert R. Carter, Member of the 11th generation of the Hill Carter family, Shirley Plantation, Charles City, Virginia

Beth Roane, Tour Guide at Tuckahoe Plantation, Richmond, Virginia

Meghan G. Hughes, Director of Collections and Interpretation, Valentine Richmond History Center, Richmond, Virginia

Kelly Kerney, Research Assistant, Valentine Richmond History Center, Richmond, Virginia

Sandy Pait, President, Board of Directors for The Rosewell Foundation, Gloucester, Virginia

Wendy K. Gay, Office Manager of The Rosewell Foundation, Gloucester, Virginia

Margaret O'Bryant, Librarian, Albemarle Charlottesville Historical Society, Charlottesville, Virginia

Connie Geary, Digital Archivist, Webmaster, and Trustee, Scottsville Museum, Scottsville, Virginia

Jennifer Belt, Associate Permissions Director, Art Resource, New York, New York

Peter Rohowsky, Art Archives, at Art Resource, New York, New York

Daisy Njoku, Archivist, Human Studies Film Archives, National Anthropological Archives, Smithsonian Institution Museum Support Center, Suitland, Maryland

J. Christian Kolbe, Archivist, The Library of Virginia Archives Reference Services, Richmond, Virginia

Jamison D. Davis, Visual Resources Manager/ Exhibit Specialist, Virginia Historical Society, Richmond, Virginia

Urbanna Historical Society, Urbanna, Virginia

Marc C. Wagner, Designation Manager and Architectural Historian, Virginia Department of Historic Resources, Richmond, Virginia

Randall B. Jones, Public Information Officer, Virginia Department of Historic Resources, Richmond, Virginia

Carol Elmore, Reference Assistant, Rockbridge Regional Library, Lexington, Virginia

Frances Allshouse, Director of Old Jail Museum, Fauquier Historical Society, Warrenton, Virginia

Timothy Hulbert, IOM, President of the Chamber of Commerce, Charlottesville, Virginia

Reverend Randall H. Haycock, Interim Rector, Grace Episcopal Church, Walker's Parish, Cismont, Virginia

Barclay Rives, Author, Cismont, Virginia

Matt Sanders, Glenmore Country Club, Charlottesville, Viriginia

Gregory Hirson, Assistant Wine Maker, Blenheim Vineyards, Charlottesville, Virginia

Andrew Ornée, Tasting Room Manager, Blenheim Vineyards, Charlottesville, Virginia

Attila Woodward, General Manager of Jefferson Vineyard, Charlottesville, Virginia

Melody Z. Day, Day Song Studios, Charlottesville, Virginia

Philip E. Day, Owner/Operator of Philip Day Communications, Charlottesville, Virginia

Renee Quesenberry-Fernandez, Partner, Mosaic Innovations in Marketing, Charlottesville, Virginia

Catherine Maino, Partner, Mosaic Innovations in Marketing, Charlottesville, Virginia

Contents

Preface 17

Introduction... 19

Prologue.. 23

Chapter I: A Respite..................................... 25

Chapter II: Jefferson, Early Surveyor........................ 31

Chapter III: Peter Jefferson, Aspiring Planter 37

Chapter IV: Planting Tobacco 43

Chapter V: William Randolph.................................. 53

Chapter VI: Peter Jefferson Marries Jane

    Randolph... 61

Chapter VII: The Loyal Land Company 67

Chapter VIII: Leaving Shadwell............................... 77

Chapter IX: Tuckahoe Plantation 81

Chapter X: Return to Shadwell 89

Chapter XI: The Dover Creek School 93

Chapter XII: Plantation Life 95

Chapter XIII: Children at Play.................................. 99

Chapter XIV: Peter Jefferson's Death 107

Chapter XV: The Maury School for Boys.............. 111

Chapter XVI: The College of William & Mary,
    First Year 119
Chapter XVII: The College of William & Mary,
    Second Year 127
Chapter XVIII: Post-Graduate Law Study............ 135
Chapter XIX: From Boy to Man 145
Chapter XX: Peter Jefferson's Legacy 153
Chapter XXI: Jane, Farewell Forever and Ever 165
Chapter XXII: Lawyer, Vestryman, Politician,
    Planter 169
Chapter XXIII: Shadwell Fire 181
Chapter XXIV: Martha Wayles Skelton 187
Chapter XXV: Courting "Patty" 193
Chapter XXVI: Married Life 201
Chapter XXVII: A Tribute to Dabney 209
Chapter XXVIII: Remembering Dabney 215
Chapter XXIX: Death and Debt 219
Chapter XXX: Earthquakes of 1774 223
Chapter XXXI: The Great Fresh of 1771 227
Chapter XXXII: August 1774 233
Chapter XXXIII: Health and Wellness 245
Chapter XXXIV: Refreshed 249

—⚏—

Peter Jefferson and Jane Randolph Jefferson
    Family Birth Dates and Cause of Deaths 253
Chronology of Events 1743-1774 255

Chart of Virginia Counties 1761-1770................... 259
Thomas Jefferson's Landholdings in Albemarle
    County, Virginia, as of 1774 261
Thomas Jefferson's Legacy
    and Accomplishments from 1774–1826 265

—ɯ—

Appendix I: The Thomas Jefferson Foundation
    and Monticello, The Colonial Williamsburg
    Foundation and Colonial Williamsburg 269
Appendix II: Charlottesville, Virginia.................... 271
Appendix III: Recipes.. 275
Appendix IV: Shadwell Today 281
Appendix V: Blenheim Vineyards,
    Charlottesville, Virginia.................................... 283
Appendix VI: The Natural Bridge,
    Natural Bridge, Virginia 285
Appendix VII: Filippo (Philip) Mazzei and
    Jefferson Vineyards, Charlottesville,
    Virginia 287

—ɯ—

References: Image Sources, Text Sources,
    Article Sources, and Web Sites........................ 295
Endnotes 327
Other Books by the Author 337

Preface

Thomas Jefferson-From Boy to Man will be enjoyed by those eager to learn, or are curious about, the early years and life events of Thomas Jefferson. It traces the ancestry of the Jefferson and Randolph families, while introducing the reader to some of the most important people who influenced Thomas Jefferson's life prior to the signing of the Declaration of Independence and the American Revolution. The book will come alive as the reader imagines colonial Virginia through the reminiscent journal entries and many rare photos from the life of Virginia's most beloved native son.

This book will be a valuable aid to teachers of history and English everywhere, and an accurate source of reference for students of Virginia colonial history. The biographical journal entries will fascinate the casual reader and Jeffersonian enthusiast, as well as those who have visited or long to visit the historical sites of Virginia.

Introduction

As a resident of Albemarle County, Virginia, I have the pleasure of living close to Thomas Jefferson's birthplace, Shadwell, as well as his mountaintop home and plantation, Monticello. Thomas Jefferson spent a lifetime gazing at the same Southwest Mountains and distant Blue Ridge Mountains, from his home, that I see every day from my own. I fell in love with the rolling hills and mountain views of Charlottesville the day my Piedmont Airlines flight touched down on December 31, 1981. Needless to say, it did not take me long to adjust to my new Virginia home. Although I am not a native Virginian, I am proud to say that I live in "Jefferson Country."

Young Thomas often dreamed of someday building his home on top of the "little mountain" that he named Monticello. I can imagine his impatience growing up, while waiting to realize his dream. Today, Monticello is protected and operated by the Thomas Jefferson Foundation. It is a 5,000-acre Palladian estate nestled in the rolling Southwest Mountains. The house still stands on the pastoral mountaintop where it is ornamented by elaborate gardens and surrounded by working farms.

Beautiful any time of year, the southern view beyond Mulberry Row stretches out over Albemarle County as far as the eye can see. Visitors especially enjoy walking beside the one-thousand-foot long restored garden terrace, then down the path to the cemetery when the grove of dogwoods and redbuds are in full spring bloom. The summer offers gentle warm breezes and luscious flowering gardens, while the fall offers changing colors and crisp mountain air. Winter, especially after a snow, is absolutely stunning, as all the leaves have fallen, allowing for an idyllic view of the town of Charlottesville and the Rotunda at Thomas Jefferson's University off in the distance. (See Appendix I.)

Visitors to Charlottesville enjoy a stroll on the Downtown Mall, shopping at the numerous boutiques, and dining at any one of the many eclectic-style restaurants. April through December, the popular Charlottesville City Market at the corner of Water and First Street, features local vendors every Saturday morning and is a shopper's delight!

One can also relax and enjoy a wine tasting at any number of local wine shops or nearby vineyards, walk the University of Virginia campus, enjoy a theatre performance or concert, or attend any one of the numerous UVA sporting events. There are many fine hotels and B&B's that beckon, and each one has perfected the art of Virginia hospitality. I would encourage you, if you have not yet visited Charlottesville, Virginia, to add it to your "bucket list." You must experience for yourself what makes Thomas Jefferson one of Virginia's most beloved sons, and the City of Charlottesville a National Award Winning City. (See Appendix II.)

As you read *Thomas Jefferson-From Boy to Man*, you will, inevitably, desire to visit Colonial Williamsburg, the 301-acre historic district of the city of Williamsburg, Virginia. The re-created colonial capital's motto, "The future may learn from the past," comes alive as you stroll down Duke of Gloucester Street, and visit the restored houses and buildings dating from 1699 to 1780. The period interpreters work and dress as they did in the era, using colonial vernacular in order to re-create the atmosphere and ideals of the 18th-century American people and revolutionary leaders. While there, you can tour Thomas Jefferson's college campus, William & Mary, visit the church he attended, eat at the taverns he frequented, locate his boarding house, and visit the shops and homes that he patronized.

I hope that by reading *Thomas Jefferson-From Boy to Man,* it will impassion you to want to learn more about the brilliant scholar, musician, surveyor, astronomer, lawyer, bibliophile, planter, architect, family man, founding father, statesman, governor, vice-president, president, scientist, and natural philosopher that was... Thomas Jefferson.

—Jayne D'Alessandro-Cox, Author

Prologue

Thomas Jefferson-From Boy to Man is a historical account of the Jefferson and Randolph family, their associations, as well as some of the most important people that influenced Thomas Jefferson's life up until August 1774.

The setting location is authentic, and the story is based on historical fact that is documented in the Reference section. What is fiction, and is the imagination of the author, is the information that places Thomas Jefferson at a specific location on the specific date of August 17, 1774, as well as the italicized journal entries in his Commonplace Book, although based on historical fact. The journal entries are not authentic quotes, although there are authentic quotes by Thomas Jefferson incorporated in the journal entries, and they are noted. The background information is factual and meant to educate the reader.

All dates in the text use the New Gregorian Calendar. The New Gregorian Calendar was adopted by Great Britain and its colonies in 1752. In order to bring the calendar in line with the solar year, it added eleven days, and started the New Year in January rather than in March.

Chapter I: A Respite

It is the seventeen-year anniversary of Peter Jefferson's death. After spending the morning visiting his mother at Shadwell and checking on the plantation's business interests, thirty-one-year-old Thomas Jefferson rides his horse, Cucullin[2], alongside the extensive tobacco field on his way back to Monticello. The tobacco is nearing harvest, and Thomas is pleased to see that the entire crop and production process had fared well over the hot summer months.

Colonial Williamsburg Historical Interpreter,
Bill Barker, portrays Thomas Jefferson
The Colonial Williamsburg Foundation

Martha is at home with two-year-old Patsy, and four-month-old Jane, and they are, no doubt, keeping their mother busy. As Thomas Jefferson rides across the rolling countryside, he approaches his favorite childhood refuge…his rock. The exposed, outcrop of greenstone is fairly flat and sprawls over a large area near a stately cluster of cedars. As a young boy, Thomas used to run off to this hiding spot when he wanted to avoid chores or escape from his younger sisters. It was a place of reflection, study, and play…where his imagination could run wild.

Greenstone Formation at Shadwell,
Albemarle County, Virginia
Author's personal photo library
Courtesy of the Monticello/Thomas
Jefferson Foundation, Inc.

Thomas Jefferson pauses at the rock and gazes out over the picturesque masterpiece beyond the weaving Rivanna. He dismounts from his horse, takes the goose feather pen, inkpot, and new Commonplace Book from his saddlebag, and places them on the greenstone slab. After hitching Cucullin to a nearby shade tree, Thomas Jefferson sits on the gently sloping mound of bedrock, and from his left-inside coat pocket, takes out the brassbound compass used by his father during his surveying days. All but memories of his father remain as he carefully inspects the instrument, surprised at its good condition and accuracy after all these years. He gently drops it back into his pocket, and begins to reflect on all the recent somber events that have occurred at Shadwell over the past fifteen months. Listening to the gentle rush of the Rivanna below, a flock of geese fly in formation directly overhead. It is a comfortably mild summer day...a day that no man should have to labor.

Somewhat somberly, Thomas allows himself a moment to reflect back on his life at Shadwell. Unhurried, he rests before returning back to Monticello, where there will, no doubt, be an afternoon of chores awaiting him. He begins to reminisce about the many memories of his youth; his boyhood adventures, the endless days at boarding school, the cherished seasons spent with his father, and the exuberant independence of his college years. But, more recently, Thomas remembers his childhood comrade, Dabney Carr, who had passed away the year prior. On this particular day, all he has is time. Thomas opens the inkpot next to him, places his notebook on his lap, and after turning to the first page, proceeds to date the top. Taking a deep breath of the fresh mountain air, Thomas Jefferson begins to write, as a gentle breeze cools him under the late morning sun.

August 17, 1774

Today is the 17th anniversary of father's passing, but it seems like an eternity since his death. I left Monticello for Shadwell earlier than usual this morning to check on the farm, visit with mother, and meet with the overseer about hiring another local carpenter to work at Monticello… Humphrey Gaines. Many of the slaves are now working up at Monticello, leaving only eighteen at Shadwell, twelve of which are children, and the others too old to work. As I sit here on my rock, I can't help but remember back to when life at Shadwell was simple, and far less demanding of my time.

Before continuing, Thomas removes his hat, places it next to him, and begins to apply pressure to his temples, hoping that his dull headache does not develop into another migraine. He takes a deep breath, exhales, closes his eyes, and tilts his head upward for a moment, allowing the warm rays of the sun to soothe his forehead. He, then, continues to write…

My loving sister, Jane, has been gone 9 years now. Elizabeth and Little Sall both died this past February in a terrible accident. Martha's father died in May of last year, as well and my dear friend, Dabney, whose death has left a void in my life, not to mention that of his children and my sweet sister Martha.

Sometimes, even though I am always surrounded by family and friends, I feel alone. I cherish my Patty, for she is a great source of joy to me and an excellent mother to our girls, but I miss the conversation with those special people in my life who knew me best… who really knew me.

Thomas puts his pen and notebook down beside him, and lies back on the rock with his hands cushioning his head. He gazes up at the summer sky and fills his lungs with fresh mountain air. Thomas' mind wanders back to memories of his father, life at Shadwell, his pioneering spirit, love of adventure, and voracious desire to learn. His eyes get heavy, and he drifts into a peaceful nap, as a mockingbird happily sings its repertoire in a cedar tree nearby.

Chapter II:
Jefferson,
Early Surveyor

For over one hundred years following the Jamestown settlement in 1607, Virginia's central Piedmont, below the hazy Blue Ridge Mountains, remained virtually a wilderness. Game was plentiful, land was lush and fertile, deer wandered in large numbers, as did bear, elk, and bison. Geese and ducks noisily paddled the ponds, and pigeons roosted in large multitudes in the forest. Grapes, strawberries, mulberries, and chestnuts all appeared to be wild. Myrtles, cedars, firs, dogwoods, red-flowering maples, sassafras, and oak trees covered the forest. Fat shad and herring swam the mountain-fed streams and rivers. The settlement of immigrants to Virginia was a slow and gradual process. Plantations were, for the most part, started on the waterways, extending along the banks of the James, the shores of the Chesapeake Bay, and its tributaries.

The first generation Jefferson to immigrate to colonial Virginia, the new colony of America, was Thomas Jefferson of Gwynedd, Wayles, sometime between the 1660s and 1670s. Born in 1653, he was of the yeoman class, a proud, industrious hard working, and independent people. There was nothing exceptional about his ancestry, but like the thousands of merchants, mariners, and traders that came to the New World, Thomas Jefferson aspired to make his money from growing tobacco. He, with his wife, Mary Branch, settled in Henrico County, in the Curles area, which was that area along the James River where its tributaries scrolled and twisted (curled) across the landscape. Thomas Jefferson was a middling planter who owned some property, as well as a surveyor who held the title of Office Surveyor of Roads from 1687 until his death in1697. His duties included laying the best routes to churches and county courthouses, as well as building and maintaining bridges.

Together, Thomas Jefferson and Mary Branch had a son in 1677, and named him Thomas. Thomas Jefferson II, later married Mary Field, was a "gentleman justice," and served as sheriff and captain of the militia. Thomas Jefferson II and Mary Field had five children: Judith, Thomas, Field, Peter (born February 29, 1708), and Mary. The Jefferson family lived in the little community in Chesterfield called Ozborne's, Henrico County, Virginia. It was a tobacco inspection station and local shipping center on the south side of the James River, now referred to as Osbornes Landing.

The surveying skills of Thomas Jefferson, Sr., without a doubt, would have an impact on the future profession of his grandson, Peter Jefferson. As a young man, he gained most of his knowledge from the practical applications learned by working on his father's tobacco plantation, and by accompanying his father on numerous business transactions.

At the age of eighteen, Peter was a strapping young man, and well prepared to manage his family's plantation. As he matured, Peter believed it to be politically and socially desirable to become more associated with the gentry on the north side of the James River. Through his parent's connections, he came to know many men of social prominence such as Thomas Randolph, and the County Surveyor Major William Mayo.

Major William Mayo was born in England, and immigrated to the British colony of Virginia, at the age of forty, in 1723. He was not only a civil engineer in Goochland County, but also a cartographer, both profitable businesses in a new country. While performing his duties as the justice of Goochland County, William Mayo realized that he needed an assistant. Being well acquainted with the Jefferson family, William Mayo hired Peter Jefferson for the job as Associate County Surveyor. Peter showed great interest in William Mayo's surveying and cartography skills, and developed a great respect for him.

As surveyors, William Mayo and Peter Jefferson, like many others of that time, were responsible for laying out the boundaries of patented public lands in order that grants and deeds for that land might be obtained by prospective settlers. Those seeking to acquire acreage were required to obtain a survey warrant from the proprietary office for a set amount of acreage in the location specified. The survey warrant, which was then issued directly from the land office to the county surveyor, instructed the surveyor to make a "just and true" survey of the land, thereby officially determining and limiting its boundaries. Once the job was completed, the survey plat and description were copied and entered into the county survey book, and the originals were sent to the secretary of state. Upon entry of the warrant, survey plat, and description, the secretary issued a land patent signed by the governor, and marked with the colony's seal.

Because surveyors were responsible for laying out the land claims, they had a unique role in Virginia society. Their appointments guaranteed a certain social prominence, since nearly all parties interested in gaining title to an area of land were required to deal with the surveyor. They were also among the most educated Virginians, and were often in the best position to purchase large estates for themselves based on their opportunities, field experience, education, and knowledge of the profession.

In Virginia, there was no formal course of study to become a surveyor. Aspiring young men could choose to read books such as *Treatise on Surveying* by John Gibson, or *Geodaesia: or The Art of Surveying & Measuring Land Made Easy* by John Love, but hands-on practice was essential. Peter learned his profession while on the job. He accompanied William Mayo on surveying trips, and received mathematical instruction from his close friend, Joshua Fry, a professor of mathematics at The College of William & Mary.

Peter's overall "education had been quite neglected; but being of a strong mind, sound judgment and eager after information, he read much and improved himself insomuch that he was chosen, along with Joshua Fry, to continue the boundary line between Virginia and North Carolina which had been begun by Colonel Byrd; and was afterward employed with the same Mr. Fry to make the first map of Virginia which had ever been made, that of Captain Smith being merely a conjectural sketch. They possessed excellent materials for so much of the country as is below the Blue Ridge, little being known beyond that ridge."[3]

Additionally, the surveyor's intimate knowledge of the land and official capacity as representatives of the King of England, or other large land holders, made their participation politically essential to large land companies, such as the Ohio Company established in 1748, the Loyal Land Company established in 1749, and the Mississippi Land Company established in 1763. Land companies, such as these, were structured to cover the costs of acquiring the land from the King of England, before leasing or selling portions of it to individual settlers at a profit to the shareholders.

Chapter III:
Peter Jefferson, Aspiring Planter

Peter Jefferson was a backwoodsman at heart who loved the outdoors, and was the very image of a frontiersman, accomplished and massive in size. He was sturdy, reliable, courageous, and with such an iron constitution that he knew no fatigue. Peter was an expert horseman and fearless rider, an impassioned sportsman, a tireless swimmer, a bold hunter, and skillful in the use of a gun, who cleared fields, and felled trees. He was a pioneering spirit who exhibited an abundance of life, and whose strength was legendary. He possessed many wilderness skills that prepared him well for the frontier culture ahead.

Peter Jefferson developed a close friendship with the young aristocrat, William Randolph, son of Thomas Randolph of Tuckahoe, and Judith Fleming. William lived on his family's 3,256-acre plantation on Turkey Island, located on the north side of the James River in the city of Henrico, Goochland County.

In 1735, William Randolph was granted 2,400 acres by King George II. The land grant was located on the north side of the River Anna, along the eastern slope of the Southwest Mountains, in the western part of Goochland County. At that time, those who invested in wilderness land, like William Randolph, were wealthy men who already had large land holdings in the eastern counties of Virginia. They did not expect to immediately occupy the land, but regarded their great patents as speculation, or a provision for their future sons.

At twenty-three years of age, and upon the death of his father in 1731, Peter Jefferson's inheritance consisted of two slaves, some livestock and horses, and some undeveloped land located upriver from Osbornes in Goochland County, which was called Fine Creek. Peter, who aspired to become a planter like his father, inherited the 1,500-acre land acquisition that his grandfather originally acquired. He moved to the Fine Creek property, cleared the land, built a house, and planted crops.

Although Peter was now the rightful owner of the Fine Creek acreage, he had aspirations of moving west. His friend, William Randolph, suggested that he investigate the fertile land along the River Anna. On this recommendation, Peter traveled northwest to explore the extensive acreage along the river, commonly referred to as the Rivanna, a northern tributary of the James River.

Peter found the bottomlands of the fertile Piedmont Region to be covered with tall grass, which, when rippled by the stiff south wind, resembled a lake of green. Far off to the west lay wave after wave of the lavender-tinted Blue Ridge Mountain chain, and to the east were their rolling foothills, the Southwest Mountain range.

The hardwood forests covered the bottomlands, and steep hillsides were broken by a few clearings of red clay dirt. Peter's encounter with the beautiful landscape was enough to convince him that he would be foolish not to acquire the available acreage, which seemed very suitable for the cultivation of tobacco.

Peter had his eye on the choice acreage along the Rivanna, in what was then Goochland County. When Peter went to file for the 1,000-acre tract, he discovered that his good friend, William Randolph, had filed two days earlier on 2,400 acres along the Rivanna, which included the 400 acres on which Peter had hoped to build his home. William, learning of Peter's dismay, promptly agreed to sell him the 400-acre tract for a fair asking price, but, at the time, Peter Jefferson did not have enough money to pay the entire amount.

In the spirit of jovial kinship, the problem was settled. Some money was put down for 200 of the 400 acres, and in good faith, William Randolph and Peter Jefferson sealed the rest of the deal over Henry Wetherburn's biggest bowl of arrack punch.

Five years later, on May 16, 1741, Peter properly paid William £50 for the remaining 200 acres to confirm the May 18, 1736 deed transfer of what would later be named Shadwell.

The financial transaction was certainly an uncharacteristic and amiable deal between two close friends, and the incident was thus preserved in the Jefferson family records. Peter began work on his future home's architectural drawings, in order to start construction the following year.

Arrack Punch, which was customarily ladled from a large bowl, combined arrack (a liqueur distilled from coconut palm sap imported from Asia or Indonesia) with sugar and fruit juice. It was commonly offered by Henry Wetherburn at the Raleigh Tavern on Duke of Gloucester Street in Williamsburg from 1731 until 1742, until Wetherburn opened his own tavern across the street. The widely popular spirit was said to cost ten shillings per quart, while French wine only cost four shillings per quart. (See Appendix III.)

The Deed for the Shadwell Estate between William Randolph and Peter Jefferson read from the Goochland County Deed Book as follows:

> By deed dated May 18, 1736 William Randolph Jun. Esq. of the County of Goochland conveyed to Peter Jefferson, Gen't. Of the County of Goochland, in consideration of Henry Wetherburn's biggest bowl of Arrack punch to him delivered, one certain tract or parcel of land containing two hundred acres, situate, lying and being on the north side of the North Anna in the Parrish of St. James in the County of Goochland aforesaid and is bounded as followeth, to-wit:
>
> Beginning at a corner black oak on the north side of the hive, thence north 23 degrees west 102 poles; thence north 64 degrees west 116 poles on the said line to a double hickory on the River shore the Sandy falls; thence down the river according to its meanders 332 pols to the beginning, and contains by estimation 200 acres be the same more or less.

Together with all houses, orchards, gardens, fences, woods, ways, waters, water courses and all other appurtenances to the same belonging or in any wise appertaining and all the state, right, title use, property, interests, claim and demand whatsoever, of the said William Randolph.

Chapter IV:
Planting Tobacco

Peter's densely wooded property eventually grew to a total of 7,200 acres. He was among the early settlers of the Piedmont area who started out farming his property and planting tobacco.

Those wealthy colonists seeking to go into the tobacco production business first needed to find large tracts of fertile soil along a Virginia waterway; the James River or any tributary thereof. The prospective planter would search for flat property along the river, laden with pines trees and sandy shorelines. Once purchased, the land was arduously cleared and prepared as a field.

The growing of tobacco in Virginia originally began as an export in the early 1600s. In May of 1609, Englishman and early American settler, John Rolfe boarded the London based ship, Sea Venture, bound for Virginia.

John Rolphe was one of many settlers sent by the investors of the Virginia Company of London, and charged with finding ways to make the English colony, founded at Jamestown on May 14, 1607, profitable. In this assignment, Rolfe was wildly successful. John Rolfe's experiments with a West Indies plant that he found in the Caribbean, nicotiano rustica (tobacco) became the first profitable New World enterprise for export. Once cultivated, the colonists found that it was a finicky crop that required a large work force. The Virginia colony steadily increased tobacco production, and by 1640, Virginia was exporting nearly a million and a half pounds of tobacco annually to London.

Virginia planters grew two kinds of tobacco, sweet-scented, worth ten pence per pound, and Oronoco, worth around two pence per pound. The sweet-scented tobacco was used for smoking, and the Oronoco, for snuff. Peter Jefferson grew the much less valuable Oronoco because sweet-scented could be grown only in the Tidewater area due to its soil composition.

Finding labor was originally a concern for the early Virginia planters, but as early as 1619, the problem was solved by importing European indentured servants, who either paid their passages or served prison sentences as "rented slaves."

The slave population in the Chesapeake area of Virginia increased significantly during the eighteenth century due to the demand for cheap tobacco labor, as well as the dwindling influx of indentured servants willing to migrate from England. The slave population began to increase to about 40 percent of the total population of the Chesapeake area, as healthy young men and women were sold from Africa and shipped as slaves to Virginia.

The preparation of the seedbeds began in January or February. Forty square yards of seedbed were required for the cultivation of each acre of tobacco. The seedbed sites were chosen, cleared, burned, and hoed. The tiny tobacco seeds were sown before the middle of March, and often mixed with sand to make distribution of the seeds more equal. The beds were raked and then covered with pine boughs to protect the emerging plants. After a month, the fragile new seedlings sprouting from the ground were thinned to approximately four inches apart.

If the new seedlings survived the spring's inclement weather and the ravages of the tobacco flea beetle, the planter would then be ready to transplant his tobacco to prepared fields in May. Knee-high hills were made every three to four feet. This task was considered the most arduous one in the tobacco cultivation process.

An experienced adult worker could prepare no more than five hundred hills a day. After hilling, the planter waited until a spring rain softened the soil and seedbeds before transplanting the tobacco plants to their final location.

Even with the best of care and weather, not all the plants would survive, and often the hills were reused to replant a new seedling until a plant eventually took. As the plant reached knee height, weekly care was necessary to protect it. The worker would hoe around each plant, reforming each mound, and eliminate any weeds or cutworms.

About two months after each tobacco plant was transplanted, a series of steps began to ensure large leaves of high quality. First, the two to four leaves growing closest to the ground were removed in a process referred to as "priming." At the same time, the small bunch of compact leaves that formed at the top of the plant was removed, in a process called "topping." This insured that the plant would not waste its energy developing flowers and seeds.

Tobacco Field
The Colonial Williamsburg Foundation

After topping, shoots called suckers emerged where the leaf joined with the stem, and were carefully removed by the worker. If this weekly process were not performed, smaller leaves would result. By this time, the tobacco plant was about three to four feet tall. Each plant was inspected daily for attacks of the feared insect, the hornworm, a small creature that also attacked tomato plants, and could destroy a crop in less than a week. The hornworms were picked off by hand and crushed underfoot.

Once the mature tobacco plants stood six to nine feet tall, usually by late August or early September, they were ready to harvest. Even if the planter had good weather and had avoided destruction by pests and diseases, his crop was still in danger. If the plants were harvested before they were fully mature, or when their peak season had passed, the crop would be worth far less.

On the other hand, if the tobacco stayed too long in the field, there was the risk of a frost destroying the entire crop. One of the skills of a Virginia crop master was the ability to judge just when the tobacco should be harvested. He would look at color (a yellowish green), texture (thick, rough and downy), and pliancy (a leaf that broke when it was folded between one's fingers).

Since the plants ripened at different times, there were numerous trips to the field during harvest. Plants were cut with a sharp knife between the bottom leaves and the ground. If the weather was favorable, the tobacco was left on the ground three or four hours to wilt. This resulted in a heavier, moister leaf that brought a higher price.

The wilted leaves were then hung on lines, sticks, or even fence rails, until tobacco barns were developed to house the crop. During this curing period, which lasted four to six weeks, the color of the tobacco changed from a yellowish green to a light tan. Since mold was always a problem, the planter relied on his experience to know when the hanging tobacco was ready to be removed from where it was hung, a process called "striking."

Once removed, the planter would wait until damp weather, and the workers then laid the leaves on the floor of the tobacco barn to "sweat" for a week or two.

Logs could be used to press the tobacco and increase its temperature, but they had to be careful that the heat generated by pressing did not become too intense and mold or spoil the crop.

After sweating, the next step was sorting. When the tobacco leaves absorbed just the right amount of moisture, they could be stretched like leather, appearing glossy and moist. If they were too damp, they would rot in transit, and if too dry, they would crumble, and be unusable and impossible to sell.

The leaves were then tied together in "hands" (bunches) of five to fourteen. The hands were returned to platforms to sweat and then prepared for shipping, once inspected by the planter. The tobacco leaves were twisted and rolled, then spun into rope, which was wound into balls weighing as much as a hundred pounds. These balls, protected in hogshead (large barrels approximately forty-eight inches long by thirty inches in diameter, having a gross weight of 1,000 lbs.), would be transported from the plantation to the nearest riverfront warehouse and tobacco inspection station on the James River, where they were weighed, inspected for quality, and stored for shipment. Once the tobacco passed inspection, it was to stay in the warehouse until it was exported.

The Tobacco Inspection Act of 1730 required that all tobacco exported from Virginia had to be inspected and meet a minimum standard of quality. All inspection stations were east of the James River fall line, the imaginary line where waterfalls and rapids drop quickly into low-lying land.

Reverend Robert Rose, a prominent tobacco planter from Amherst, Virginia, initiated the first commercial navigation in the Piedmont region in 1747. Before using the rivers to transport their product, the planters used oxen to roll the hogsheads to market, which was both slow and expensive. Robert Rose devised a rather unique method of lashing two canoes together with a board platform in between, which enabled eight or nine hogsheads of tobacco to be rolled onto the vessel, and carried on the James River. This became known as the "Rose method." It was reasonably stable and especially suited to the tobacco hogshead containers.

These "double dugout" canoes were fifty to sixty feet long, and were later known as "tobacco canoes" or "tobacco boats." Hogsheads filled with tobacco could then be transported to the nearest inspection station, and be transported by river using the double dugout method in order to reach its market in Richmond. There, the hogsheads were loaded on to ships and exported to England. (This method was replaced in 1771 by the batteau.)

From Shadwell, Peter Jefferson would use oxen to transport his tobacco hogsheads a few miles down Three Notch'd Road toward the village of Charlottesville, across the Rivanna, where it was traded to Scottish merchants at their factor store/tobacco warehouse, and stored. In an era when paper money and coins were almost non-existent, tobacco growers, like Peter Jefferson, brought their crop to the Scottish merchants in exchange for a store certificate, or tobacco warehouse receipt. There he would then trade for finished goods from Europe, at any one of five to six Scottish factor stores along the Rivanna, which together generally stocked hundreds of items available for sale or trade.

Factor Store Certificate/Tobacco Warehouse Receipt
Special Collections, John D. Rockefeller, Jr. Library
Colonial Williamsburg Foundation

The Charlottesville factor stores and tobacco warehouse were located just over the Rivanna, where Free Bridge on Virginia State Route 250 is located today, and was found to be a very convenient location for planters throughout Albemarle County to carry their tobacco. The Scottish merchants stored the tobacco in their warehouse and eventually transported the hogsheads to the James River, by way of the Rivanna.

Although Peter did not get as much for his tobacco in comparison to what he would have gotten on his own at Scott's Landing, present day Scottsville, he did not have to worry about transporting it there.

The James Mills Scottish Factor Store on the Rappahonnock River in Urbanna, Virginia, was originally built in 1766. It is one of the oldest surviving mercantile structures in America associated with the sale of tobacco. It exemplifies the colonial trade pattern of exchanging tobacco for various items imported from Europe.

Factor Store or "Old Tobacco Warehouse"
James Mills Scottish Factor Store on the
Rappahonnock River, Urbanna, Virginia
Courtesy of Dave Lipscombe, L! Marketing
& Design, Mechanicsville, Virginia

Before the emergence of the Scottish factors, tobacco and other crops where shipped directly from large plantations to England in exchange for goods on the return voyage. The Scots established stores where tobacco was exchanged immediately for cash and credit with which to purchase imported goods for sale.

Evident of the knowledge necessary to be a successful planter, and the labor-intensive work of the plantation worker, tobacco buyers understood that behind every crop of "good" tobacco was a meticulous planter with a skilled labor force. The tobacco production industry eventually became Virginia's primary export throughout the colonial period.

Chapter V:
William Randolph

Upon Thomas Randolph's death in 1729, his son, William, inherited Tuckahoe plantation on the James River in Goochland County, and it was there he would build his home.

The name Tuckahoe is derived from the Algonquin word "ptuckweoo," translated to describe the aquatic and bog plants that provided starch in the diet of the American Indians. The Indian women would search the freshwater riverbank marshes for the arrow-shape leaf plant, pull out the roots, pile them up, and smoke them. They were then pound into a starchy powder, and used to cook bread. Before the Indian corn was ready for harvest, the Indian women cooked the "ptuckweoo" root out of necessity, in order to feed their families.

In 1736, William Randolph met and eventually won the hand of the fifteen-year-old heiress, Maria Judith Page, the second child and only daughter of Mann Page of Rosewell, in Gloucester County, and his wife Judith Carter.

Newly wedded, William brought Maria to his plantation home at Tuckahoe, which was situated on a bluff overlooking the James River. The early Georgian-style home was originally a relatively small, wooden, two-story rectangular structure, unpretentious, with shapely cornices, classically molded trim, and a plain gabled porch, surrounded by landscape and soaring trees. Maria had been left a dowry of £2000 sterling upon her father's death, part of which the newlywed couple devoted to constructing an addition to the already existing home in preparation for their future family and many guests. The addition included a central salon and a two-story south wing, besides an English basement that was used as the kitchen. The house was completed in 1740.

Dendrochronology, or tree-ring dating, indicates that the present Tuckahoe mansion was built in two sections and at two different times, the original north wing in 1733, and the central salon and south wing in 1740, while William Randolph was residing there.

The front entrance to the house faces north, and looks up the cedar-lined, one-mile long plantation entrance. When the Randolph's were residing there, one entered the house by climbing four granite rock steps. Today, these same steps lead up to a wooden porch, under a small plain gabled roof supported by simple wooden posts. Each side of the porch is framed by a wooden railing and dark sashed windows.

Entering through the front door, the rooms on either side of the staircase, as well as the central salon, are paneled with the more expensive black walnut. Yellow pine wood flooring is laid throughout the entire house, which includes the original north wing and second floor bedchambers, the attic, the central salon, and the south wing. It is presumed that the skilled carver who completed the interior woodwork of Maria's family mansion, Rosewell, also completed the north wing's intricately carved staircase and richly embellished interior woodwork.

West View of Tuckahoe House
Author's personal photo library
Courtesy of the Tuckahoe Plantation, Richmond, Virginia

The long, two-story central salon has two exterior doors that lead out to the yards on each side of the house. The north-front exterior door looks up the entrance from the road, while the south-rear exterior door and yard overlooks the James River in the distance. The north wing's exterior was built entirely of wood with a brick exterior chimney, while the south wing and central salon were built of wood, but with a brick end wall and interior chimney. Tuckahoe became a two-story, sprawling white, H-shaped wooden home, with a gabled roof, displaying wings mirroring each other.

Approximately twenty yards to the east of the main house is the schoolhouse that Peter Jefferson built for the Randolph and Jefferson children, and beyond the schoolhouse, a flat grass yard and the English box-wood maze garden. The family cemetery is located just behind the boxwood maze garden.

Approximately twenty yards to the west of the main house is the overseers office, and behind it, the herb garden. The old kitchen, smokehouse-storehouse, and stable are located down what is called the plantation street, which runs parallel to the front yard. The slave quarters were often located in outbuildings near the plantation street, and referred to as the "home quarter." As a working plantation, Tuckahoe's shoreline tract was one of its most valuable assets.

William and Maria had three children together, but did not long enjoy their genteel newly-renovated mansion at Tuckahoe. Unfortunately, Maria died in 1742, prior to her husband, who followed her to the grave in 1745. (Visit www.tuckahoeplantation.com.)

Mann Page, Maria's father, was a prominent Virginia planter, the second largest landholder in Virginia, and an appointee to the Governor's Council in Williamsburg. His wife, Judith Carter, was the daughter of the wealthiest man in the colonies, Robert "King" Carter of Corotoman Plantation on the Rappahanok River in Lancaster County.

Mann Page and his family lived at Rosewell, a magnificent thirty-five-room mansion on the banks of the York River, which started construction in 1725 and was intended to rival and exceed the Governor's Palace in Williamsburg in size and luxury. Due to Mann Page's untimely death in 1730, he would neither live to see his daughter, Maria Judith, marry William Randolph, or the completion of Rosewell in 1737.

Rosewell Mansion, circa 1875
Courtesy of The Rosewell Foundation,
Gloucester County, Virginia

The 12,000 square foot mansion was primarily constructed of brick, marble, and mahogany, and stood three stories tall. It had a large reception hall and lofty ceilings, which was indicative of its refined taste and wealth. From the upper windows, a magnificent view included the surrounding level lands and the creeks leading to the York River. Rosewell was a place of grandeur and importance, and hosted the area's most posh balls and parties. (Visit www.rosewell.org)

Judith Carter's father, Robert "King" Carter, was a Speaker of the House of Burgesses, Treasurer of the Virginia colony, a member of the Governor's Council, and later became President of the Governor's Council. He was Rector of The College of William & Mary, and Governor of Virginia between 1726 and 1727, and was nicknamed "King" due to his wealth, political power, autocratic business methods, and the thousands of acres of countryside that he cultivated near Richmond. Upon his death, his estate consisted of forty-eight working plantations, 1,000 slaves, £10,100 sterling, and over 330,000 acres of land, which included the Shirley plantation in Charles City County.

Shirley Plantation on the James River Courtesy of the Shirley Plantation, Charles City, Virginia

Today, Shirley plantation is open to the public, and stands as the oldest of the great plantations along the James River, tracing its roots to the establishment of the earliest English Settlement in the New World. (Visit www.shirleyplantation.com.)

Chapter VI:
Peter Jefferson Marries Jane Randolph

Jane Randolph's father, Isham Randolph, was born at his family's estate and plantation, Turkey Island, Virginia, around 1690. "They trace their pedigree far back in England and Scotland."[4] He was educated in the Virginia colony at The College of William & Mary in Williamsburg. While living in England for a time, merchant and sea captain Isham Randolph met and married his wife, Jane Lilburne Rogers, in Bishopsgate Church, London. According to the Jefferson family Bible, young Jane Randolph was born on February 9, 1720, to Captain Isham Randolph, and his wife, Jane Rogers.

Barely able to make ends meet in Shadwell, a poor-crowded maritime neighborhood on the River Thames, Isham, took his wife, young daughter Jane, and infant son Isham, and sailed back to Virginia to partner with his brother in the shipping business. This move occurred sometime between August 1724 and October 1725.

At that time, a transatlantic trip from England to Virginia could take between forty-eight and sixty-three days, depending on the winds and weather. It was not an easy trip. Even if they made good time, they endured close and crowded quarters, the pitching and rolling of the vessel, perils of choppy seas, and foul drinking water. Many ships had problems with rats and worm infested, spoiled, or scarce provisions. Passengers who did not suffer from sea sickness, could not escape from those who did, and the ships were infamous containers for deadly diseases such as smallpox.

Map of Transatlantic Voyage, circa 1700
Tate Publishing Illustration Department

The Transatlantic route followed a clockwise flow of winds and currents. The ship sailed south from England, past Spain and Portugal, and stopped over at the Madeiras, Canary Islands, or Cape Verdes, for food and water before attempting the long Atlantic crossing. In the absence of major obstacles, this leg of the voyage usually took ten to fourteen days. Then, with the northeasterly trade winds and the equatorial current at their backs, the ship voyaged to the West Indies. An uneventful crossing usually required four to five weeks.

After replenishing supplies once again, they picked up the Gulf Stream and followed it northeast from around the Strait of Florida, to the latitude of Roanoke, Virginia...a trip of another ten to fourteen days. (Ships sailing from Virginia back to England usually took the Gulf Stream and the North Atlantic Drift to Europe, perhaps with a stop in the Azores for provisions. Being more direct, the homeward voyage back to England usually took much less time.)

As the ship entered the Chesapeake Bay at the mouth of the James River, young Jane saw a heavily wooded shoreline, broken intermittently by plantations and small settlements. While their home was being built, Captain Randolph, Jane, and their two young children, lived on Turkey Island, in Henrico County, about twenty miles from Williamsburg.

By 1730, young Jane and her parents, brother, and two small sisters moved to their new home, named Dungeness, in Goochland County, land bequeathed to Isham by his father, William Randolph. Throughout their marriage, Isham and Jane (Lilburne Rogers) Randolph would have nine children: Jane, Isham, Mary, Elizabeth, William, Thomas, Anne, Susanna, and Dorothy.

Isham had many brothers, all of which were bequeathed land up and down the James River. Tuckahoe was one such property settled by Isham's brother, Thomas Randolph, and located ten miles from

Dungeness. Thomas Randolph later bequeathed the Tuckahoe plantation to his son, William Randolph, Peter Jefferson's friend.

By 1737, Peter Jefferson, along with some of his highly skilled slaves, journeyed from his home at Fine Creek to his newly acquired Rivanna property to begin clearing the land in order to build his future family's homestead. Through his acquaintance with William Randolph, Peter met Jane Randolph, William's charming and talented seventeen-year-old cousin, and daughter of William's wealthy Uncle Isham Randolph.

Peter was one of many suitors for Jane's attention, and after a two-year courtship, the thirty-two-year-old charismatic Jefferson won the nineteen-year-old's hand in marriage. They married at the Randolph plantation home, Dungeness, on October 19, 1739, just fifteen miles from Peter's home at Fine Creek.

Although her influence was not strong, Jane brought family connections to the marriage, besides the "promise" of a £200 dowry. Peter Jefferson, who had already achieved some social status, became more prominent upon marrying Jane Randolph. Upon his death in 1742, Isham Randolph's estate had accumulated so much debt that the £200s set aside as Jane's dowry was, instead, needed as payment toward his debts. Therefore, Jane Randolph was unable to bring a dowry or property into the marriage.

As husband and wife, Peter and Jane, after spending some time at Dungeness, accumulated their personal belongings, bid their family farewell, and set out to Peter's property on the Rivanna, at what was known to be the edge of the wilderness.

Jane inspired her husband to name their property Shadwell, after the parish where she was born and christened, outside of London, England. The parish register at St. Paul's Church, Upper Shadwell, notes her baptism on February 25, 1721, as does her family Bible.

Jane immediately became pregnant with their first child, and on June 27, 1740, a daughter, Jane, was born. Their second child, Mary, was born on October 1, 1741. The Jefferson's home at Shadwell was a work in progress, until early June 1742, when construction was finally completed.

The following December, while the Jefferson's were residing at Shadwell, the Virginia General Assembly passed an act forming two more Anglican parishes in Goochland County; Fredericksville to the north of the Rivanna, and St. Anne's to the south. As new residents of the community north of the Rivanna, Peter Jefferson and his family would now belong to Fredericksville Parish.

The Shadwell home site was nestled in the middle of a ten-acre square clearing, on a rise of ground, atop a gently sloping hillside. The simple wooden house faced south with a view of the Southwest Mountains from their front yard. While the rolling green stretch of Piedmont beyond the Rivanna was to the west, and the back of the house faced Three Notch'd Road to the north, Shadwell commanded a sweeping view of the entire countryside.

Peter was in his mid-thirties when he and Jane's third child and first son, Thomas, was born on April 13, 1743, a time of the year when the dogwood buds opened and the wild honeysuckle bloomed. He was named after his father's paternal grandfather and great grandfather, both named Thomas Jefferson. The magic of the beautiful land, Shadwell, would have a lasting influence on the mind of their first son.

Chapter VII:
The Loyal Land
Company

In 1619, the House of Burgesses was created in order to provide a representative government under the Virginia Charters. As a natural extension of the English Constitution, it assisted the Governor in making laws to enhance the conditions in the colony, and make life more agreeable for its current inhabitants and growing population.

By 1740, there weren't more than thirty counties in Virginia. The House of Burgesses was the only branch of the colonists' political system that was made up of elected officials, and at that time, consisted of only sixty-three men. Each county was allowed to elect two representatives as members of the House of Burgesses. The city of Williamsburg, James City, and the College of Williams & Mary, were only allowed one representative due to the size of their population. If you were a free white male, Protestant, and a landowner, you were eligible to be elected to represent your community. The members were selected from Virginia's aristocracy and served at the command of the British crown.

House of Burgesses, Capitol Building, Williamsburg
Reenactment of Patrick Henry's "Caesar-
Brutus" speech and his defiant resolutions oppos-
ing the Stamp Act, May 15, 1776
The Colonial Williamsburg Foundation

Back in 1634, one of the original English counties was Henrico County. As the Virginia colonies thrived, and emigration poured in from England, Ireland, Scotland, and Wales, the population moved west, forming Goochland County in 1728.

So many settlers had eventually moved into the western sections of Goochland County that on September 18, 1744, the House of Burgesses passed an act dividing Goochland County into two separate counties. The eastern half remained Goochland, named after Lieutenant Governor William Gooch, and the new western half was named Albemarle County, after the Royal Governor-General William Anne Keppel, the second Earl of Albemarle.

Like many early settlers, Joshua Fry was an extensive land holder who earned a living through surveying and selling land, as well as being one of the land speculators and charter member of The Loyal Land Company. He was dedicated to opening up as much land as possible to English settlement.

Joshua Fry was born about the year 1700 in Somersetshire, England. On March 31, 1718, at the age of eighteen, he matriculated from Wadham College with the great advantage of an Oxford education. As a young man of twenty-one, he emigrated from England to Essex County, Virginia. By 1731, he had started a boy's grammar school attached to the College of William and Mary, and later chaired the college's math department. He gained further political prominence serving as a member of the House of Burgesses, and as a justice of the peace for Essex County.

Like many young men of colonial Virginia, Joshua Fry made a fortune by marrying well. In 1737, he wed Mary Micou Hill, the widow of a wealthy plantation owner from Spotsylvania County. By 1744, he moved his wife and family to one of the westernmost reaches of Virginia, an 800-acre plantation bordering the Hardware River, called Viewmont, in hopes of taking advantage of unpatented lands and surveying opportunities in the area.

Viewmont was approximately four miles north of the growing town of Scott's Landing on the James River, present day Scottsville, and ten miles south of the small town of Charlottesville. Today, you can still see what's left of the chimneys of the original home, from Virginia State Route 20.

Viewmont, home of Joshua Fry, Scott's Landing (Scottsville), Virginia. Historical American Building Survey, Bagby. The Albemarle-Charlottesville Historical Society, Charlottesville, Virginia

As Albemarle County had just been founded, with Scott's Landing as the county seat, Joshua Fry was named Magistrate, Chief County Surveyor, and Colonel for the militia. As Chief County Surveyor, Joshua Fry was responsible for finalizing claims on tracts of land throughout the county. At the time that Colonel Fry was named the Chief County Surveyor of Albemarle County, he appointed his close friend and neighbor, Peter Jefferson, as the Assistant County Surveyor. When Joshua Fry was elected Colonel of the Albemarle County Militia, Peter was immediately appointed Lieutenant Colonel, and Peter was thereafter referred to as Colonel Jefferson. There were other appointments as well, namely Colonel William Randolph of Tuckahoe, who was named County Clerk.

In March 1745, Peter Jefferson was commissioned, along with his good friend Joshua Fry, to create the new county lines for Albemarle County, as well as become a member of the first county court in said county.

In early September 1746, Peter and Joshua Fry, again, teamed up to survey the Fairfax County line of the Northern Neck. Once the data was collected from the expedition, the plat based on William Mayo's earlier map was drawn up, while Peter added topographic features, such as the Shenandoah Valley and the Blue Ridge and Allegheny Mountains.

On December 12, 1749, Peter Jefferson was requested to attend a meeting in Albemarle County with other local surveyors and land speculators, to discuss the forming of a new company dedicated to exploration. It was called The Loyal Land Company. The management and direction of the company centered on John Lewis, the founder, who appointed Dr. Thomas Walker as the company's agent for exploration, along with the other surveyors and new charter members, Peter Jefferson, Joshua Fry, Reverend James Maury, and Thomas Turpin, Sr., to name a few.

On July 19, 1750, Acting Governor Lewis Burwell and his Council appointed Peter Jefferson to, again, team up with fellow surveyor, Joshua Fry. The two men were commissioned, by warrant, to explore, survey, and create a comprehensive map of the 800,000-acre

Virginia Colony, to include the bays, navigable rivers, counties, parishes, and principle estates.

By this time, Fry and Jefferson were experienced surveyors who had already worked together to create the Albemarle County lines in Virginia's Piedmont region in 1745, the Fairfax County Line in 1746, and to extend the western portion of the boundary line between Virginia and North Carolina in 1749. The pressure to produce a map of the Virginia Colony compelled Fry and Jefferson to rely on their own surveys and experiences to supplement existing published maps, manuscript maps, and field notes.

The survey required that they lay chains across an uninhabited and inhospitable countryside, as well as file the final draft within four years. Starting from a spring in the Blue Ridge Mountains, down into the Shenandoah Valley, the way was easy; afterward the surveyors climbed and descended range after range of the Allegheny Mountains to reach the headspring of the Potomac. Despite difficult terrain and conditions, the surveyors persevered.

In 1751, the final drafting of the comprehensive survey map of the 800,000-acre Virginia Colony was then delivered to Acting Governor Lewis Burwell, who then forwarded it to the Counsel. The Counsel examined the map and could not differentiate between Fry's or Jefferson's hand; it was done in such accord.

The map later became known as the famous Fry-Jefferson Map "of the Most Inhabited Parts of Virginia", and was renowned for its accuracy.

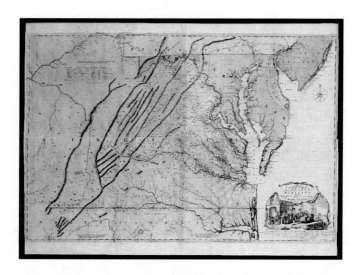

Fry-Jefferson Map
A Map of the Most Inhabited Part of Virginia
by Joshua Fry & Peter Jefferson, London, 1768
The Colonial Williamsburg Foundation, Museum Purchase

The Fry-Jefferson Map became the definitive map of Virginia in the eighteenth century, and Joshua Fry and Peter Jefferson became well known for their cartography and surveying skills. The map contained the whole province of Maryland, part of Pennsylvania, New Jersey and North Carolina, and included the completed border survey for the western bounds of the Northern Neck and a portion of the Virginia-North Carolina dividing line.

For the first time, the entire Virginia river system was properly delineated, and the Allegheny Mountains were accurately depicted, as well as "The

Great Waggon Road to Philadelphia". Published in eight known editions, the map was widely copied, and served as an important resource for future mapmakers. Today, a copy of the original Fry-Jefferson map hangs proudly on the wall of the entrance hall at Thomas Jefferson's Monticello.

In 1753, The Loyal Land Company also began the preliminary planning for an expedition up the Missouri River to the Pacific Ocean due to the enthusiasm of settlers wanting to move west. Thomas Walker was to lead the expedition, but the adventure never took place because the French and Indian War intervened.

Ten-year-old Thomas Jefferson heard about this expedition from his father and his tutor, Reverend James Maury. It would not be until Thomas Jefferson was President of the United States in 1803, sixty years later, that he would commission the Lewis and Clark Expedition to explore the Northwest Territory in order to observe a transcontinental route, as well as to provide important information on the native people, plants, animals, and the geography of the explored land.

Thomas Walker, lead member of The Loyal Land Company, was born in the Tidewater area of Virginia, and was raised as an Englishman. As a young man, he attended The College of William & Mary, studied medicine and became a physician. Thomas Walker began his career as a doctor, but later changed his profession to surveying, which at that time gave better prestige and financial returns.

At age twenty-six, Thomas Walker married a widow, Mildred Thornton, who had acquired 15,000 acres of land in Albemarle County from her late husband's estate. In 1765, the couple built their home known as Castle Hill, a 600-acre plantation located at the foot of the Southwest Mountains in Albemarle County, where they started their family and became prominent in the community.

Castle Hill, home of Dr. Thomas Walker
Sketch of original clapboard colonial residence, built 1765.
The Albemarle-Charlottesville Historical
Society, Charlottesville, Virginia

Chapter VIII:
Leaving Shadwell

Thomas Jefferson's nap is interrupted by a squawking crow flying overhead. He opens his eyes and sits up, wondering how long he had dozed off. As billowy clouds slowly pass across the azure sky, shading Thomas from the early afternoon sun, he continues to write.

> *Although I was too young to remember all the circumstances, it happened that Mother's cousin and father's dear friend, William Randolph, became very ill in the latter part of 1745. William's wife, Maria, had died in 1742, leaving him a widower with three young children. At that point, William felt the need to draw a will insuring that his children would be properly cared for, and specified how they should be educated in the event of his own untimely death. In his will, William named father and mother as guardians of his children, requesting that father move east to Tuckahoe plantation with our family, and remain there until his only son and heir to the family name, Thomas Mann Randolph, became of age.*

While sitting at his desk at Tuckahoe, William Randolph, in a codicil to his will wrote, "Whereas I have appointed by my will that my dear only son Thomas Mann Randolph should have a private education given him in my house at Tuckahoe, my will is that my dear and loving friend Mr. Peter Jefferson do move down with his family to my Tuckahoe house and remain there till my son comes of age with whom my dear son and his sisters shall live."

For Jane, there were advantages to moving to Tuckahoe. The house was grander than her Shadwell home, and it was much closer to her friends and family at Dungeness, ten miles away.

> *William Randolph died at age 33, leaving behind two daughters and one son; 9 year old Maria Judith, who we called Judy, 7 year old Mary, and Thomas Mann, who was two years older than me. In honoring Mr. Randolph's exceptional request, my father agreed to move our family to Tuckahoe, and become guardian to the orphaned Randolph children, as well as manage the Randolph family's plantation. I was raised to "believe that every human mind feels pleasure in doing good to another,"[5] and although it was a personal sacrifice and commitment, Father was pleased to honor his dear friend's request.*
>
> *In our absence, father hired managers to run Shadwell, while the enslaved continued to work under them. With the help of visiting family members, the hired help, and slave labor, Shadwell remained an active plantation. Father assumed his role as resident executor of Tuckahoe, as well as custodian in charge of the care and rearing of the*

young Randolph children, while still pursuing his surveying duties.

"My earliest recollection of Shadwell goes back to when I was two years old. I remember being handed up to a mounted slave, and carried comfortably on horseback, while riding on a pillow."[6] Father led the way, followed by my horse. Six-year-old Jane, five-year-old Mary, one-year-old Elizabeth, and mother, pregnant with Martha at the time, rode in the coach-and-four behind me, along with our family's belongings. Four servants followed up the rear. I was told that Father was concerned about the wheels of the coach, due to the rough condition of the trail. There were tree roots to ride over, and in many areas, rain formed large pools of water, eroding the well-traveled road even further.

We continued down the mud track Three Notch'd Road until we reached our destination, 50 arduous miles east of Shadwell. Once we arrived at Tuckahoe, I remember father taking me off my horse, and carrying me into the house. When I was older, I remember father explaining to me and my sisters that what kept us from getting lost in the wilderness were the chopped notches in the trees along the trail, made by the Indians and earlier trail blazers.

For many years, the Monacan Indians, pioneers, and travelers had worn a hunting path into the popular dirt road known as Three Notch'd Road by hacking three notches into the bark of trees along the trail. In colonial times, the road originated in the village of Charlottesville, extended east to Henrico County (present day Short Pump), and west from Charlottesville to Wayland's Crossing (present day Crozet) in Albemarle County. It was first called the Mountain Road when Peter Jefferson surveyed it in 1734. The road closely follows the original path of the early settlers, who also referred to it as the King's Highway, and then later called it Three Chopped Road. In the mid-19th century, the spelling later changed to Three Chopt Road, which synonymously became known as Three Notch'd Road, or the Richmond-Albemarle Passage. Since the 1930s, it has been referred to as Virginia State Route 250, or Richmond Road.

> *Not long after arriving at Tuckahoe, on May 29, 1746, mother gave birth to my sister, Martha. During our stay at Tuckahoe, mother gave birth to Peter in 1748, but he unfortunately died after one month. Another son was born in 1750, and died at birth, unnamed.*

Chapter IX:
Tuckahoe Plantation

At Tuckahoe, the Jefferson children were raised to the same standards of conduct that the parents knew. Jane Jefferson taught her children etiquette and the social rituals that would someday allow them to occupy elevated status in Virginia. The Jefferson children grew up with refinement, manners, and were well behaved. They took dance lessons and learned country dances, reels, and the more formal minuet. Music was an important part of the social life in colonial days, and most well-educated children had musical training at an early age. The Jefferson children learned how to read music and to play a musical instrument, such as the spinet, harp, or fiddle.

Mrs. Jefferson was described as having a peaceful nature, with a cheerful temperament, gentle manners, and a lively humor. She ran the household, was a good organizer and was accustomed to delegating work to the household servants that worked in the main house and elsewhere around the plantation. Peter continued to travel extensively on surveying trips to remote corners of Virginia to support his family.

Being the youngest member at the plantation,
I was sometimes bullied by my three cousins and

often preferred to play with the slave children, who were amongst my earliest friends, or my sister Jane. I always enjoyed listening to Jane play the spinet, and appreciated her loving patience as she taught me how to read music.

Jane's music tutor was very strict, and instructed her to practice her lessons for long periods of time. The longer she practiced, the lonelier I was without her. I remember asking Jane if she would teach me how to read music so we could spend more time together, and she agreed. Father came home with a fiddle for me one day, and from then on, Jane and I spent many hours practicing our lessons together.

While Jane played the spinet, I played my fiddle, and together we would sing my favorite hymnal Psalms 57 and 148. I was said to have a pleasant voice, and frequently sang to myself while I walked about. Singing seems to calm my nerves, and it passes the time on my various travels. Eventually receiving music instruction myself, "I suppose that during at least a dozen years of my life, I played no less than three hours a day."[7]

Father "placed me at the English School at five years of age,"[8] joining my older sisters and cousins in the small one-room schoolhouse next to the main house. One tutor, Thomas Staples, made us memorize our basic lessons in English grammar and spelling, and write the alphabet on our writing slates with chalk.

Tuckahoe Schoolhouse
Author's personal photo library
Courtesy of the Tuckahoe Plantation, Richmond, Virginia

The slave children at Tuckahoe were not allowed to attend school, but had to work in the fields planting, weeding, and watering the gardens. At a very young age, I had witnessed mean spiritedness toward the slave children by some adults, as well as, at times, the other children. Although I was fully aware of the hierarchies of power between black and white children, the injustice always seemed to disturb me.

Without being directly taught, children on plantations throughout the colonies became aware of the subtle hierarchies of power between black and white children. At an early age, Thomas learned that whites ruled over blacks, but it did not stop him from extending friendship to them. He also learned that only white children went to school, and only white children had to study. This seemed to disturb him as being unfair, and he would write, later in life, about the injustice of white children's tyranny on the plantation in his *Notes on the State of Virginia*, Query 18, 1781.

With remarkable sensibility, Thomas Jefferson's *Notes on the State of Virginia*, Query 18, 1781, states,

> "There must doubtless be an unhappy influence on the manners of our people produced by the existence of slavery among us. The whole commerce between master and slave is a perpetual exercise of the most boisterous passions, the most unremitting despotism on the one part, and degrading submission on the other. Our children see this, and learn to imitate it; for man is an imitative animal.... The parent storms, the child looks on, catches the liniments of wrath, puts on the same airs in the circle of smaller slaves, gives a loose to his worst of passions, and thus nursed, educated, and daily exercised in tyranny, cannot but be stamped by it with odious peculiarities. The man must be a prodigy who can retain his manners and morals undepraved by such circumstances."[9]

It is logical to understand how Thomas Jefferson would later embrace the rationalism and philosophy of the Enlightenment movement of the eighteenth century, the period of intellectual excitement and optimism which was marked by the rejection of traditional social, religious, and political ideas of that day. Written down by interviewer Reverend Charles Campbell in 1847, seventy-year-old Isaac Granger Jefferson, as a free man living and working as a blacksmith in Petersburg, not far from Pockahontas bridge, quoted vivid recollections by stating, "Old master very kind to servants."

> *Although I loved to read and write, I disliked going to the schoolhouse, and believed the studies to be rigorous. I remember one afternoon, I slipped out of class and hid behind an outbuilding, in hopes that mother would soon call me in for supper.*
>
> *Along with all the school work, there was always time for fun. Jane, Mary, and my cousins would often roam around the gardens and outbuildings. We especially enjoyed fishing for crawdads in the shallow creek down below the herb garden. We would then take the bucket of crawdads and head down to the James River to fish. When the creek froze during the winter months, we would slide all along the ice until our shoes were drenched.*

On a nice day, the children at Tuckahoe enjoyed playing simple games outside, and there was always a rolling hoop nearby. They loved to play Blind Man's Bluff, commonly called tag, in the English boxwood maze garden, which was filled with flowering shrubs and beds of flowering perennials. Fox and Geese was another popular game played on the ground with carved wood pieces or pebbles.

On cold or rainy days, the children played cards and board games inside the house. The Cup and Ball toy was a favorite childhood amusement. Nine-Men-

Morris was a simple old English game that made its way to the colonies with the new settlers. It was played with black and white pebbles on a board marked out with chalk. Adults and children enjoyed playing other board games together such as the Game of Goose and Mankala. Some of the games were easily made at home, while others would have been purchased from a local merchant.

Mother often entertained invited guests and passing visitors at Tuckahoe. At meal time, there were always a large variety of delicious foods on the table. Much of the food was prepared in the outbuilding on plantation street, and taken to the kitchen below the dining room of the south wing. The food was placed in pewter-covered platters and pulled up through the dumb waiter, then transferred on to dinner dishes by the household servants, who politely served us around the dining table.

For breakfast, coffee was offered to the adults, while milk was poured for the children. We often enjoyed hot cakes with bacon, and bread with apple butter was always on the breakfast table. Midday dinner consisted of cider, a deep-meat pie, corn bread, roasted chicken, fried oysters, peas, potatoes, sweet potato fritters, pickles, bread and butter.

I always looked forward to dessert, which consisted of small sweet items such as oatmeal or Shrewsbury cakes, custard, a variety of fruit tarts, and my favorite ginger cakes. Later in the evening, we would have a brief supper of bread, cheese, hasty pudding, and warmed-over meat from the noon meal.

My family belonged to the Anglican Church of England, and as was our custom, we were all baptized as infants. By the time I was five years of age, I had learned to recite the Lord's Prayer, and I can still remember Jane trying to teach me the words. Neither of us understood its meaning, but she helped me memorize it non-the-less. On Sunday afternoons, we had to memorize scripture and read the Bible, which was the only book we were allowed to read on Sundays. As I grew up, I retained a familiarity with the Bible regarding all its psalms, hymns and prayers.

In colonial times, education was not a priority for girls, but they did need to know how to read, write, and do a little arithmetic. Girls were taught how to spin, weave, knit, and sew, and they spent long hours practicing their music. They were expected to keep house, and often took care of the servants when they were sick.

Before bedtime, Jane and Mary would sit by the fire and sew, I would write my lessons, while mother played with Martha. When it grew too dark in the ½ hour before the candles needed to be lit, we would play Charades or word games. One such favorite was called, "I Love My Love With an A." The first player began by reading a sentence, and filling in each blank with a word beginning with an "A." The next player did the same thing with a "B," and so on through the alphabet.

While the Jefferson children were safe under their mother's care, Peter Jefferson was often gone on long surveying trips for weeks and months at a time. Being away from the comforts of Tuckahoe was not easy. Peter and his fellow surveyors had to hunt deer, bear, or squirrel just to eat, and sleep on the ground when oftentimes there was not adequate shelter to protect themselves from rain or wolves. There was so much excitement when the children saw their weary and hungry father riding down the cedar-lined lane of Tuckahoe. Jane and the children would all run out to welcome him, while the servants tended to his horse.

Chapter X:
Return to Shadwell

Tuckahoe offered me many privileges and opportunities, but I had a hunger to return to Shadwell, as did mother, and I often expressed my sentiments to her. Although my family did not stay at Tuckahoe as long as Mr. Randolph desired, my parents guarded the plantation and children for seven years before finally returning home to Shadwell. Before leaving, Father made sure that Thomas Mann, who was 11 at the time, was well taken care of, and that the plantation was in good hands.

We arrived back at Shadwell in August of 1752, and found our home and many of the out buildings in disrepair. By then, Jane was 12, Mary was 10, I was 9, Elizabeth was 7, and mother was seven months pregnant with Lucy. My parent's seven year absence took a toll on our house. Father immediately began making the necessary repairs to bring our home back to its original condition, as well as added a porch and increased its size to accommodate our growing family.

Peter Jefferson's income as a surveyor enabled him to enlarge the original-modest wood frame home, as well as add a dairy, a smokehouse, and outbuildings. The hilltop home soon developed into a 1,600-square-foot, sophisticated, spacious, weather-boarded one-and-a-half-story farmhouse. It had a wooden chimney, a wide entry parlor, a kitchen, a library/office where Peter displayed his maps and shelved books, a dining room, and a master bedchamber with two closets on the main level. The upstairs attic was divided into two bedchambers under a shingle roof, and was large enough to sleep five to six people to a room, as well as two to three in a bed. Below the house were the brick root and cooling cellars. (See Appendix IV.)

Eighteenth-Century Gristmill
Tate Publishing Illustration Department

The Jefferson home, in the middle of the cleared ten-acre square, would soon become the domestic center of the plantation. Built within this acreage were the dwellings, out buildings, icehouse, slave quarters, a charcoal kiln, various shops and barns, stables, vegetable and flower gardens, and orchards.

Beyond the ten-acre square lie the tobacco fields, pastures, and forestland. The land sloped southward for several hundred yards to the Rivanna, where Peter built a gristmill to grind wheat, and a brewery. He even erected a sundial to track the hours of the day. Young Thomas was mentally taking notes, as he learned by observing and helping his father around the growing plantation.

The house and landscape matched Peter Jefferson's professional work and social life. Peter kept the books, ran the farms, and managed all the business dealings, from transactions with neighbors to his transatlantic tobacco commerce, while Jane took care of the household and children, as well as took great interest in gardening. She supervised the digging of the terraced garden behind the house, while she taught the children how to plant her favorite purple hyacinths, and yellow narcissus, as well as the profusion of other fragrant and showy flowers such as irises, carnations, marigolds, violets, hollyhocks, poppies, and snap dragons.

Peter Jefferson owned such livestock as horses, cattle, pigs, and sheep on the extensive property that loomed over the Rivanna. Chickens were raised for their eggs and meat, as well as turkeys. The vegetable gardens were laid out in numbered beds, each row designated by a letter. Peter grew asparagus, spring peas, celery, Spanish onions, lettuce, radishes, broccoli, cauliflower, and cucumbers. In the orchards were trees that bore cherries, gooseberries, plums, strawberries, and walnuts.

Peter Jefferson's plantation produced enough food to feed his family and the working slave population.

In 1754, Peter was elected to represent Albemarle County in the Virginia House of Burgesses. Colonel Peter Jefferson was well respected in his community as a western Piedmont landowner. He was a successful businessman primarily due to sales from his prosperous wheat and tobacco crop, which were the principal exports of commercial agriculture.

By then, double dugout canoes were traveling on all the tributaries of the James River, which would include the Rivanna, and Peter Jefferson was well on his way to becoming a tobacco planter. His Shadwell farm was doing well, the tobacco had been planted, and he had the slave help and vision to succeed. For decades the market price of tobacco had been about two cents a pound, but severe droughts in 1759 and 1760 drove the price of tobacco much higher to six pennies per pound.

The Jefferson's were doing well financially, but only somewhat wealthy in comparison to the vast majority of free Virginian's who lived in one-room houses, and often times with dirt floors. Peter Jefferson, though, was a very good provider for his family, unfortunately spending weeks, and sometimes months, at a time away from home on surveying jobs, while Jane was accustomed to being left in charge at home.

Chapter XI:
The Dover Creek School

At nine years of age, father arranged for me to be tutored by Anglican minister, Reverend William Douglas, at his Latin boarding school, Dover Creek, located near Tuckahoe; while sisters Jane, Mary, and Elizabeth were schooled at home. "My teacher Mr. Douglas a clergyman from Scotland was but a superficial Latinist, less instructed in Greek, but with the rudiments of these languages he taught me French."[10]

When father delivered me to the Dover school, Reverend Douglas introduced me to the other boys boarding there. We studied, ate, and played together, and in no time at all, we were best friends. For the next five years, I was taught a classical education, read English literature, received instruction in music, and became very skilled at playing the violin. It was at the Dover School that I first learned to keep a notebook, which was later strongly encouraged by my law instructor and mentor, George Wythe…a habit that I have continued to this day.

At twelve years old, Thomas was still attending the Dover Creek School. He was only allowed to return to Shadwell for Christmas holidays and during the summer months. A break from school represented a vacation, a reunion with his kin, horseback riding, hunting, fishing and swimming on the Rivanna, and a chance to play with his sister, Jane, and his slave friends. If there were a huge pile of hay, Thomas would jump in it. If there was a maple tree to climb, he would, no doubt, climb it.

Thomas enjoyed daydreaming at his favorite rock about someday living on top of his little mountain just on the other side of the river. His adventure hunts took him through the dense forest, and often times, he would hear the echoes of the gobbling wild turkeys, the snarling cry of a bobcat, or the rustling of a startled deer in the thicket.

Chapter XII:
Plantation Life

Between October 1739 and October 1755, Jane Jefferson was pregnant almost 50 percent of the time, having her first child in 1740 and her last, a set of twins, Anne and Randolph, in 1755. She did not nurse her infants. Old Sall, a slave woman who bore her own children about the same ages as Jane's, was the wet nurse for the Jefferson children.

By 1757, Peter Jefferson was the second largest slaveholder in colonial Albemarle County, recording sixty slaves at the Shadwell plantation. The one-room slave quarters were located down the hill, as the dirt path curved toward the river. The male slaves worked outside planting and tending the tobacco and crops, caring for the livestock, and clearing the fields for pasture land as part of their regular tasks. They worked in the dairy, storehouse, blacksmith shop, barn, garden house, and smoke house, which extended east and west of the main house along the ridge. They also worked in the gristmill and the brewery down by the banks of the Rivanna.

In the spring of 1757, Peter Jefferson and his slave help built the first known dam, mill, and millrace, the man-made canal, which allowed the river water to flow to and from the mill wheel.

Peter Jefferson had many well-trained slaves. Sandy was a shoemaker, but since he also possessed jockey skills, he worked with the horses. Sawney, a mulatto slave and the father of Old Sall's children, was Peter Jefferson's valet. He was in charge of all Peter's personal needs, and was also a trained shoemaker along with Sandy. Sampson and Jupiter worked with broadaxes to dress the lumber at the mill. Phill was a wagoner. The other slaves worked as carpenters, coopers repairing barrels and casts, blacksmiths, tailors, and shoemakers.

Making handcrafted pipes from the local stones phyllite/schist or soapstone, and smoking tobacco were hobbies for the male slaves, as well as some of the women slaves. During times of relaxation, they played dominos, and marbles made of clay, on the flat dirt surface. The women would make jewelry from strips of leather, glass beads, and shells.

Jane Jefferson emphasized a well-ordered home from the slave women who worked inside the house, and delegated that they do the laundry, clean the house, and dress and care for the children. In the kitchen, they prepared all the meals, and were taught to pickle, sugar, salt, smoke, and dry foods to keep them from spoiling.

A common family breakfast at Shadwell included eggs and bacon, bread, a bowl of porridge, cider or milk for the children, and tea or coffee for Jane and Peter. Dinner, around mid-day, was fairly large, and could consist of smoked turkey or fried chicken, possibly fish caught from the Rivanna, bread, corn fritters, a variety of vegetables from the garden, and pudding. When Peter Jefferson's work day was over, Jane would have supper ready for him and the children, which might have been warmed-over meat from the noon meal, bread, cheese, and for Peter, home brewed beer.

Each slave received a pair of shoes and had two outfits per year. Slave women were in charge of quilting, knitting, and spinning. They hand wove their summer garments from a natural coarse linen material made from the fiber of the flax plant, and home spun coarse wool and hemp to make their garments for the winter months.

Shadwell was fully equipped with everything a prominent Virginia family might need or want. Jane Jefferson had grown up in a home of refinement and hospitality with the latest imported luxuries ordered directly from ship captains. She carried this tradition to Shadwell, entertaining with her imported housewares from Bristol, England. Jane's guests were offered freshly brewed coffee from a silver coffee pot, tea from her blue and white Chinese porcelain, or punch, all served from one of three tea tables in the front hallway. During their stay, guests enjoyed imported wine or cider, as well as fancy imported foods to satiate their appetite. In the evening, their home was alive with music and filled with the aromas of good food. Thomas learned much about hospitality from watching his mother welcome people into their home.

Most Virginia plantations were isolated from each other by stretches of dense forest and wretched roads. Shadwell, however, was up the hill from the public highway, Three Notch'd Road, the country's main east-west thoroughfare, and was a "stopping place for passers-by."[11]

> *I remember when father had come back from one of his surveying trips, and my parents invited Joshua Fry and his family, from Viewmont, to stay for a long weekend. We all listened to father and Mr. Fry's stories of their many hardships; the near starvation of their horses, repeated falls, perils of fighting off animals and snakes, the constant danger of climbing over rocks, crawling through brush, and wading through icy streams. They told us how they would build a fire around themselves to keep the wild animals away at night, and how they often slept in trees for safety. Father taught me how to persevere in the face of danger, but more importantly, how privilege brought with it a duty to one's country.*

Thomas also admired his father's political savvy, and someday hoped to follow in his father's footsteps. Being the oldest son, Thomas was expected to take over the family business at the plantation, and his father began grooming him in that direction, just as his father did for him. But the young man had loftier dreams, and knew that an education was his right of passage to realizing them.

Chapter XIII:
Children at Play

It is moments like this that I miss my sister Jane, who, as I recall, always wore her sun bonnet outside when we played. We shared a love of nature, often venturing out beyond the front yard gate to pick wildflowers in the high grass. Just a stroll from the house, over the hill, and along the tobacco field, rests the large outcrop of smooth bedrock where I now sit. We would pretend that this rock area was our fort, and that the small surrounding cedar trees were soldiers guarding our fortress.

Jane and I were most happy when we were down by the river. We blazed through briars and underbrush on our way to the river bank, where we would pretend to be explorers on the mysterious Mississippi. I was always curious as to what type lands laid beyond the great Mississippi. Father often told me that the land was not surveyed, but the Indians used to tell me that it was mainly grasslands and desert. As a young boy, I often dreamt of navigating the Mississippi and exploring the vast territory beyond it.

Rivanna at Shadwell, Virginia
Author's personal photo library

Neighbors to Shadwell were few and far between, and those that were in the area were largely Native Indians. As lieutenant colonel of the Albemarle County Militia, Peter Jefferson had established a good relationship with the peaceful Cherokee Indians, while others who lived near the Jefferson family did not welcome Native Indians, and in many cases, were terrified of them. Cherokee tribes would pass through the Jefferson property along the forest paths from Tennessee on their way to the colonial capitol of Williamsburg. It wasn't unusual for as many as one hundred Cherokees to camp within the ten-acre square of the house and down along the Rivanna, doubling the population of Shadwell for as long as two days.

Peter Jefferson extended kindness and hospitality to Chief Ostenaco (also referred to as Chief Outecite Outassete, or Austenaco), the great warrior and orator of the Cherokee people, who occasionally stopped at the Jefferson home to obtain permission to camp on the property. Chief Ostenaco was always welcome at their meal table, which helped create a mutual respect and friendship between both men. Like his father, young Thomas admired the dignity, strength, and intelligence of the Cherokee people, and observed many of their unusual and fascinating customs.

Cherokee Chief Ostenaco (Outecite) wearing the silver gorget, a gift from King George III, July 1762
National Anthropological Archives,
Smithsonian Institution

Cherokee Indian Chief Ostenaco was born in 1703 in Polk County, East Tennessee. He was the warrior chief of the Cherokee town Tomotley, a historic Native Indian site in what is now Monroe County, Tennessee. As a young boy, he lived in the Appalachian Mountains, and quickly learned the arts of warfare, which earned him the honored title "Mankiller," the second-highest rank in the Cherokee military system and equivalent to a colonel in the British system.

For many years, Chief Ostenaco proved himself to be one of the greatest warriors in the entire Cherokee nation. During colonial times, he and his people relied on European goods such as clothing and gunpowder, and understood the importance of trade. When traveling traders began leaving his area due to attacks by bands of other hostile Indians tribes, Chief Ostenaco and a force of forty-seven warriors began patrolling routes to protect them.

In November 1761, twenty-six-year-old Lieutenant Henry Timberlake led a diplomatic journey down the Holston River and up the Little Tennessee River to the towns of the Overhill Cherokees in order to explain a peace treaty. In the village of Tomotley, he was greeted by Chief Ostenaco. After spending three months with the Cherokees, Lieutenant Timberlake and Chief Ostenaco became friends. The Chief's daughter became pregnant with Timberlake's son, and the child would later be named Richard.

Henry Timberlake and Chief Ostenaco traveled back to Williamsburg together in the spring of 1762, accompanied by about seventy-two Cherokee Indians.

There, Chief Ostenaco approached Governor Francis Fauquier and expressed his desire to meet King George III. Eventually it was decided that three of the Cherokees, an interpreter, and Timberlake would make the journey to England in May 1762. While studying in Williamsburg, Thomas Jefferson and fellow student, Mann Page, Junr., went to listen to the grand farewell speech that mighty Chief Ostenaco gave to 400 of his people, outside Williamsburg, on the eve of his voyage to England. Although Thomas and Mann did not understand a word uttered, they were filled with awe and veneration at the chief's articulation, animation, and the reverent silence of his people.

Lieutenant Timberlake, Chief Ostenaco, Chief Cumnacatogue, and Chief Pouting Pigeon arrived in England and were greeted with much pomp and fanfare. Thousands of English residents, who had never seen a Native Indian, were extremely curious to see the three newcomers. Their visit was a popular media sensation with their every move being recorded. Unfortunately, their bilingual interpreter had died at sea coming over, which resulted in difficulties in their communicating with the English. The Cherokee chiefs were finally able to meet the 24-year-old King George III in July, and were each presented with a silver gorget, a piece of ornamental collar armor intended to protect the throat, inscribed with their name.

Months later, King George III issued his famous Demarcation Line Proclamation, and for a while, the Cherokees and other Indians west of the Appalachians breathed easier, for English colonials were, for a time, forbidden to encroach upon their lands.

Chief Ostenaco returned home a hero, and remained especially close to his beloved grandson, Richard Timberlake. In 1765, Lieutenant Henry Timberlake died a pauper at age 30, as a result of paying many of the expenses for the three chiefs to travel. Chief Ostenaco died in Ultiwa on Ooltewah Creek (today known as Hamilton County, Tennessee) at age 73, in 1780.

The Three Cherokees (Chief Ostenaco, Chief Cumnacatogue, and Chief Pouting Pigeon) Published by George Bickham, London, circa 1765 Special Collections, John D. Rockefeller, Jr. Library, The Colonial Williamsburg Foundation

After supper, father would allow me and Jupiter to visit the Indian camp, but only when there was

a full moon. We would sit around their crackling fire as sparkling embers rose up beyond the flames like lightning bugs. We watched as Chief Ostenaco raised his arms and chanted to the Great Spirit God. I observed how much he cared for his people and likewise, saw how much his people respected and loved their leader. Many despised the Indians as barbarians, but father and I found them fascinating fighting men, and worthy of great respect.

The slave children at Shadwell closest to our ages were Jupiter, Peter, Jesse, Ada, Ephrey and Aggey. Jane and I would play with them down by the new water mill, dig worms for bait and fish along the bank. During the summer, when the river was at its lowest, we would fish from the boulders that bridged the river. At certain times of the day, when the angle of the sun was just right, the Rivanna glistened like candles flickering on a Christmas tree.

Chapter XIV: Peter Jefferson's Death

On June 25, 1757, father took ill, and mother sent Sawney, father's man servant, to Castle Hill to request the services of our family friend, Dr. Thomas Walker. By July 13, father's health was not improving, and on that day, father wrote his will and appointed Dr. Walker as one of the executors for his estate. The other men he appointed were friends and business associates, Thomas Turpin Sr., John Nicholas, John Harvie, and mother's cousin, Peter Randolph.

Dr. Thomas Walker and Thomas Turpin Sr. were partners with Peter Jefferson at The Loyal Land Company. John Nicholas and John Harvie were investors with Peter in a speculative land development and Peter Randolph was a lawyer and the family's legal counsel in charge of handling the estate's legal affairs. All were large land and slave owners who promised Peter and Jane that they would take care of any estate representation and family guidance. Although these men had access to a network of relationships that would help pave the way for young Thomas to take his rightful place amongst the gentry, Thomas could not help but feel the void of his father's presence.

Peter Jefferson's Will stated: "…I do appoint Constitute & Ordain the Honorable Peter Randolph Esq., Thomas Turpin the Elder, John Nicholas, Doctor Thomas Walker & John Harvie Execrs of this my last Will & Testament & Guardian to all my Children in Testimony whereof I have signed sealed & Published this as my last Will and Testament. I give and devise to my dear & well beloved wife Jane Jefferson for and during her natural life or widowhood the use and profits of the house & plantation whereon I now live."

Father requested to be buried at Shadwell, and hired local carpenter Samuel Cobbs to build the coffin. Dr. Walker made eleven visits to Shadwell before father passed away at age 49, just 17 years ago today. The traditional funeral service was performed by the Rev. Mr. James Maury, and afterward, my beloved Father was buried at Shadwell amongst the graceful cedars.

"…Father died August 17, 1757, leaving my mother a widow"[12] at age 37. He provided well for mother by leaving her the house and plantation at Shadwell for her lifetime, together with a sufficient portion of slaves, stock, and horses. To the estate, he left speculative land holdings, rental properties, and unlike many of his peers, no debt. After 17 years of marriage, mother was left with eight children ranging from ages 2 through 17, and now in charge of running the family plantation.

I was on summer break from the Dover School at the time, but due to the circumstances, would never return. I revered my father, and realized that I would now have to become the man of the family. "But thrown on a wide world, among entire strangers, without a friend or guardian to advise, so young too, and with little experience of mankind, your dangers great, and still your safety must rest on yourself...I recollect that at 14 years of age, the whole care & direction of myself was thrown on myself entirely, without a relative or friend qualified to advise or guide me..."[13]

This comment casts a curiously slanted image of Thomas' mother, whom he apparently did not judge qualified to advise him. Thomas would not receive any portion of his inheritance until the age of twenty-one, and was subject to the scrutiny from the executors of the estate, Dr. Thomas Walker and John Harvie, as well as his mother. Thus, at fourteen, he was now head of the family with all its many responsibilities, but he had no power.

The adolescent years are a time when boys normally struggle with parental control and begin to assert their authority. The troubled teen had no masculine companionship within the immediate family after the death of his father. He had his mother, six sisters, and an infant brother. Due to the fact that Peter Jefferson was away on surveying trips much of the time, and young Thomas had been sent to boarding schools for his education, quality time with Thomas had been more the norm than quantity time. Bereaved Thomas felt that he had been deserted at the age of fourteen. In his Commonplace Book, Thomas protested his mother's authority and brooded about his father's death. He wrote about being friendless, alone, and suffered under the hands of women.

Chapter XV: The Maury School for Boys

After father passed away, I never returned to the Dover School. In times of loneliness, I found myself in the company of local troubled youths, and became concerned that I may be influenced too much by their bad behavior. Mother observed my need for guidance and recognized that I required mentoring by respectable men. Father's last wishes for me were that I would have better opportunities than he had, and left instructions for mother to further my education, which allowed me to get relief from my troubles at Shadwell.

At 14 years old, Mother arranged for me to board at the home of the Rev. Mr. Maury, a good friend of father's, and attend his school called the Maury School for Boys. It was near enough to Shadwell that I could return home on weekends. I would describe the Rev. Mr. Maury as "...a correct classical scholar, with whom I continued two years."[14] He required that all his students keep, what he called, a literary Commonplace Book. In it, we wrote notes from the Greek, Latin, and English literature texts, in order to have them available for memorization and study. It was at the Maury School that I met my best and long-time friend, Dabney Carr.

James Maury was born in Dublin, Ireland, on April 8, 1717, and in that year migrated with his family to Virginia. James Maury was educated at The College of William & Mary in the School of Philosophy, and upon his graduation in 1741, he sailed to England to study at the divinity school. He was ordained as an Anglican minister of the Church of England in 1742. As a newly appointed clergyman, Reverend Maury would be a man of authority, supported by parish tithes, and respected by all.

In the same time period, across the ocean, the Virginia General Assembly had passed an act forming two more Anglican parishes in Goochland County; Fredericksville to the north of the Rivanna, and St. Anne's to the south. In Fredericksburg Parish, three new Anglican churches were established: Buck Mountain Church, Middle Church, and Trinity Church. Whoever pastored this parish would have to travel the clay dirt roads quite a distance to deliver his sermon between the three churches.

After returning from England to the colonies, Reverend Maury became a minister in King William County for one year. He married Mary Walker, a cousin of Dr. Thomas Walker, and it is believed that through the new family connections, he was offered the job as pastor of Fredericksville Parish in 1751, which included the three churches it served, Buck Mountain Church, Middle Church, and Trinity Church. Reverend Maury and his wife moved to their home in Albemarle County, at the foot of the Southwest Mountains, close to Dr. Walker's Castle Hill and not far from the Middle Church.

In colonial times, it was customary for clergymen to supplement their income by teaching. Reverend Maury followed that trend by conducting a classical school for boys called the Maury School for Boys, which was independent of the Middle Church that he pastored. The Maury School was a small one-room log school-house that was built on his property, four miles east of the Middle Church. When Thomas boarded there in 1757 and 1758, the students were Thomas, Reverend Maury's son Matthew, Dabney Carr and three other local youths. Reverend Maury charged £20 a year to the parents of each student.

Clergymen of the established Anglican Church of England, like other public officials in colonial Virginia, received their annual salaries from the government, which was set forth by the colonial legislature. Clergymen were paid by the government in tobacco, receiving 16,000 pounds of tobacco per a year as their salary.

Upon Reverend Maury's death on June 9, 1769, his body was buried under the pulpit of the Middle Church site where he had preached for eighteen years. Today, his grave is marked by a stone obelisk, surrounded by a wrought iron fence, outside from the front entrance of Grace Episcopal Church, on Jefferson Highway (Virginia State Route 231) in Cismont, Virginia.

Reverend James Maury Grave and
Original Site of Middle Church
Grace Episcopal Church, Walker's Parish, in background
Author's personal photo library
Courtesy of Grace Episcopal Church Vestry
Jefferson Highway, Cismont, Virginia

*Dabney was born on October 26, 1743, the same
year as I. He was raised at Bear Castle, a 1,000
acre farm in Louisa County, by his parents John
and Barbara Carr. Dabney and I shared much
in common and immediately became very close
friends. For two years under the Rev. Mr. Maury,
we studied classics, manners and morals, mathematics, literature, philosophy, natural science, history, and geography, which the Rev. Mr. Maury
felt was one of the essential features in the education of well-rounded young gentlemen.*

During the two years that I boarded at the Maury School, I traveled home on weekends to help mother and to visit my siblings. When I was not doing chores, I would hike throughout the mountains hunting for squirrel, wild turkey, rabbit, quail, or partridge. Being around nature has always been a peaceful refuge for me, as it offers relaxation as well as adventure.

Nicknamed "Long Tom," Thomas Jefferson was slim, at six feet two and a half inches, which was tall considering that the average man at the time stood five feet six inches tall. In later years, his slave, Isaac Granger Jefferson, who worked as a tinsmith and blacksmith at Monticello, described his master as being a tall and straight-bodied man with square shoulders, long face and a high nose. His cheeks were lean and his jaw square and firm. Thomas had auburn to light-red hair, fair skin that freckled and sunburned easily, pointed features, and deep-set hazel eyes. He expressed fluent, humorous, and pleasant conversation in a low voice, but could also be shy and reserved. He was described as being the perpetual charmer, and usually made an excellent impression upon both men and women.

Thomas had a great love for reading and writing, and often had a book in his hand. He knew his Bible, and continued to love and become proficient in the English classics. The young scholar was able to read Greek and Latin authors in their original text. Because of his unusually high intellect, Thomas was greatly influenced and encouraged by Reverend James Maury, and long-time friend of the family, Joshua Fry, to apply to The College of William & Mary.

> *At age 16, I realized that if I continued to live at Shadwell, after being exposed to the life at Tuckahoe, Dover Church and the Maury School, I would never have amounted to much. I would probably have become an idler if I stayed at home, like so many of my local friends did. I often felt enslaved at Shadwell, and considered my life to be "a dull monotony of a colonial subservience."[15] The wasting of precious moments disturbed and frustrated me. I often enjoyed reading and studying, and Shadwell did not lend itself to that. It was then that I decided that the best way to improve my mind and strengthen my character was to go away to college.*

The Shadwell library was small in comparison to that of Tuckahoe and Dover Church. Thomas was looking forward to moving away from home, and began to give serious thought to enrolling at The College of William & Mary in Williamsburg, Virginia's capital and education center.

After a discussion with Peter Randolph, Thomas argues for permission to enter the College of William and Mary with Dr. Walker of Castle Hill and John Harvie of Belmont, the Jefferson estate executors and his respected guardians. John Harvie, the active executor of Peter Jefferson's estate, was the person responsible for providing Thomas with the estate funds necessary for college tuition and personal spending money.

In a letter written on January 14, 1760 to John Harvie, one of the earliest preserved Jefferson letters, Thomas stated his reasons for wanting to go to college. He wrote,

> "Sir, I was at Colo. Peter Randolph's about a Fortnight ago, & my Schooling falling into Discourse, he said he thought it would be to my Advantage to go to College, & was desirous I should go, as indeed I am myself for several Reasons. In the first place as long as I stay at the Mountains, the Loss of one-fourth of my Time is inevitable, by Company's coming here & detaining me from School. And likewise my Absence will in a great Measure put a Stop to so much Company, & by that Means lessen the Expences of the Estate in House-Keeping. And on the other Hand by going to the College I shall get a more universal Acquaintance, which may hereafter be serviceable to me; & I suppose I can pursue my Studies in the Greek & Latin as well there as here, & likewise learn something of the Mathematics. I shall be glad of your opinion, and remain, Sir, your most humble servant, Thomas Jefferson, Jr."[16]

Today, John Harvie's Belmont mansion is no longer, but, during Thomas Jefferson's time, it was located across from Shadwell, off of Three Notch'd Road, and stood contiguous to the present day home at Edgehill Farm, which rests on the summit of a gentle hill crowned with lofty cedars and oaks.

Chapter XVI:
The College of William & Mary, First Year

It was decided. At nearly 17 years of age, I would be attending classes at the prestigious College of William & Mary. Dr. Walker had assured me that he would watch over my family and Shadwell while I was away. Jupiter helped me pack my belongings and load up the phaeton, then we left Shadwell for the 120-mile trip to Williamsburg.

In December of 1759, I bade good-by to my family and we took the long road to Williamsburg, stopping midway at the little town of Hanover, on the Pamunkey River. There, I stayed at the 6,000-acre plantation home of the wealthy shipbuilder, Colonel Nathaniel West Dandridge, and enjoyed a very festive Christmas season with wine, punch, laughter and dancing. It was there that I met the amusing 23-year-old Patrick Henry, and we became well acquainted.

Once the festivities were over, we left Hanover and arrived William & Mary on the 25th of March. I settled Jupiter in at the Assembly-house, then entered the Wren Building and paid my first

> *year's tuition at the Bursar's Office. I registered*
> *with the School of Philosophy, and was assigned*
> *courses in physics, metaphysics, mathematics, rheto-*
> *ric, logic, and ethics. I chose to live on campus,*
> *and resided on the 3rd floor of the Wren Building*
> *with the other boys, instead of accepting an offer to*
> *live at the grand house of mother's cousin, Peyton*
> *Randolph, located on the corner of Nicholson and*
> *North England Streets. I wanted to be independ-*
> *ent, and not under the watchful eye of my relatives.*

The College of William & Mary is the second-oldest college in America, and was closely affiliated with the Church of England throughout the colonial period. On February 8, 1693, King William III and Queen Mary II of England signed the charter for a "perpetual College of Divinity, Philosophy, Languages, and other good Arts and Sciences" to be founded in the Virginia Colony. Construction of The College Building began in 1695, and was completed in 1699, with the addition of the Chapel wing being added in 1732. The College Building is currently called the Christopher Wren Building, named after Sir Christopher Wren, one of the most highly acclaimed English architects in history, and is the oldest academic building in English America. (Visit www.wm.edu/)

The Wren Building included the library, the chapel (left wing), and the great hall (right wing). The students were served meals in the great hall, as well as attended large gatherings, lectures, and recitals there. The second floor served as the quarters for the masters and administration, while students resided on the third floor. The passageway, or gallery, was a gathering place for students and faculty between classes. The view from the piazza, in colonial times, would have been pasturelands, out buildings, and woodlands. The outbuildings consisted of the kitchen, laundry building, and stables.

WILLIAM & MARY COLLEGE, WILLIAMSBURG, VA.

Print
Sir Christopher Wren Building
College of Williams & Mary
Lithograph by Crump after a painting
by Thomas Millington, circa 1850.
The Colonial Williamsburg Foundation. Museum Purchase.

During Jefferson's stay, The Reverend Thomas Dawson was the President of The College, while the entire black-gowned faculty consisted of seven men: The Rev. Emmanuel Jones, master of the Indian School; The Rev. Thomas Robinson, in charge of the grammar school; The Rev. William Preston, professor of moral philosophy; The Rev. John Camm, professor of theology; The Rev. Richard Graham, preacher of natural philosophy; Dr. William Small, professor of natural philosophy and mathematics; and George Wythe, Esq., professor of law. By 1760, there were probably less than a hundred faculty and students altogether, and both were expected to live and work within the Wren Building.

In addition to the school of philosophy, the collegiate course in which Thomas Jefferson enrolled, The College of William & Mary, as mentioned, included a grammar school, a divinity school, and an Indian school. The grammar school, a prep school for the college, was for boys between the ages of twelve and sixteen years of age, who were strictly disciplined in Latin, Greek, mathematics, and penmanship. The divinity school was for young men who had completed their studies in the philosophy school, and desired to prepare for ordination in the Church of England. The Indian school was founded for the education and Christianizing of Indian boys.

I ate communal meals in the great hall, and did my morning and evening prayers in the chapel. Every Sunday, I attended Bruton Parish Church, located on the corner of the Palace Green and Duke of Gloucester Street. I sat with the other students in the rear gallery. College faculty and members of the House of Burgesses sat with other dignitaries on the north side of the aisle, while the women and their children sat on the south side. The enslaved people, who had permission to attend from their masters, sat on benches in the back of the church, while their children sat on the floor.

The Bruton Parish Church
The Colonial Williamsburg Foundation.
Gift of Vestry of Bruton Parish Church

Bruton Parish Church, of the Church of England, was formed in 1674 by the merger of two earlier parishes, and took its name from the town of Bruton in county Somerset, England. Governor Alexander Spotswood designed the building in 1711, and the General Assembly and its parish funded the construction. Completed four years later in 1715, the church was seventy-five feet long with fourteen-foot transepts extending out each side. An addition in 1752 lengthened the chancel twenty-two feet, and gave the church its symmetrical cross-like form. By 1754, a brick wall enclosed the area, the baptismal font arrived in 1758, and the Tarpley Bell Tower was erected in 1769. Bruton Parish Church has been in continuous use since the days when church and state were united in Virginia, and represents the established Anglican authority in the colony.

> *During my first term, I joined, and was one of the six members of the Flat Hat Club, which was a secret college society devoted strictly to fun. The F.H.C. truly "had no useful object,"[17] but had a charitable purpose.*

The Flat Hat Club, F.H.C, was first formed at The College of William & Mary on November 11, 1750, and was the forerunner of the American Fraternity system that we have today. For students of the philosophy and the divinity school, the college calendar year was divided into three terms: **Hilary Term** began the first Monday after Epiphany (January 6th) and ended on the Saturday afternoon before Palm Sunday (late March). A two-week Easter break then commenced until the Sunday after Easter (late March/early April). The **Easter Term** began that Monday and ended on the eve of the Sunday before Whit Sunday, also known as Pentecost, (mid-May). They had a two-week break until Trinity Sunday, currently known as the first Sunday after Pentecost (late May). **Trinity Term** began on that Monday and ended the eve of St. James's Day (July 25th). A three-month summer break then began until St. Luke's Day (October 18th). Classes resumed on October 19th until December 16th, when a four-week Christmas break commenced. The students were not expected back for their 2nd semester until the Hilary Term began in early January.

It seemed, for a time, that I became greatly influenced by my association with the young and rowdy freshman, besides being influenced by my youthful temptations, gaiety, and frivolity. We patronized any one of the five taverns in Williamsburg: Chowning's, Raleigh, Wetherburn's, King's Arms, or Shields, my favorites being Chowning's alehouse near Market Square and the Raleigh Tavern, closer to the Capitol building on Duke of Gloucester Street.

The Raleigh Tavern was the most famous Williamsburg hostelry, dedicated to Sir Walter Raleigh, who took a leading part in sending colonists to the New World. The Raleigh Tavern was popular for its lodging and meals, and was a center for social activity, as well as such business activities as public auctions of land, slaves, and goods. Plain meals were served to hungry travelers and local residents on sturdy dishes of pewter and salt-glazed stoneware. The meals were prepared in the kitchen and bakery, a separate building from the tavern itself. Servants carried the food across the courtyard into the tavern where most customers paid a fixed price for the meal of the day, which would have consisted of meat or fish, vegetables, bread, perhaps fruit, and beer. Tavern keepers also prepared special meals for those renting a meeting room. Eighteenth century diners enjoyed sweets such as custard, fruit-filled tarts, bread and jelly, pies, and cakes. The innkeeper also served as postmaster to both transients and townspeople, who would claim their messages from the crisscrossed ribbons tacked to the wall.

Raleigh Tavern
The Colonial Williamsburg Foundation

I was happy to be at college, and considered William & Mary to be "the best school of manners and morals in America."[18] On Saturdays, I went to the horse races, attended balls, and almost never traveled without my chess set and fiddle. It was in Williamsburg that I developed a keen interest in the arts, and attended numerous theatrical events with friends in the Apollo Room at the Raleigh Tavern.

On weekends, John Page, my cousin and a fellow classmate, frequently invited me to his family's magnificent estate, Rosewell. On a clear night, I remember how we climbed many flights of stairs to the attic in order to access the mansion's great lead roof. There we spent untold hours gazing at the stars and sharing our love of astronomy.

Chapter XVII:
The College of William
& Mary, Second Year

When I returned home to Shadwell after the first summer, I realized how much time I had wasted and money I had spent on merriment and clothes my first year at college. While visiting with Dr. Walker at Castle Hill, I offered to repay my first year's tuition of £13, out of my own pocket, because I felt that I had wasted the trust money.

Thomas Jefferson's trust from his father's estate paid The College of William & Mary Bursar's Office £13 for each of the two semesters, March 1760 to March 1761, and March 1761 to March 1762. Thomas was also charged £1, 1 shilling, and 8 pence for the remaining month March 1762 until his graduation on April 25, 1762. In Old English money, 12 pence (12p) = 1 shilling (1s), and 20 shillings (20s) = 1 pound (£1). Pence is plural for penny.

But my wise guardian said, "If you have sown your wild oats in this manner, the estate can well afford to pay for it." I was grateful for his understanding, and vowed to be more responsible with the

*trust money by becoming a more serious student
and studying much harder in the semester to follow. Dabney Carr had also enrolled at William &
Mary, and he returned back to college with me in
hopes of later studying law.*

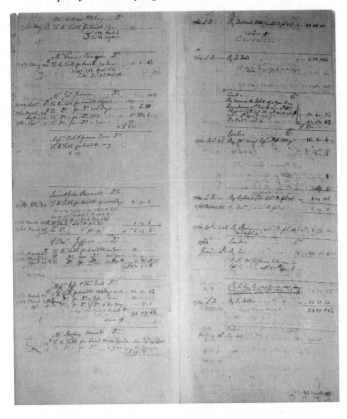

Thomas Jefferson's Tuition Entry 1762-1763
College of William & Mary Office of the Bursar
Records, Special Collections Research Center
Earl Gregg Swem Library, The College of
William and Mary, Williamsburg, Virginia

1761_March 25th	To the Table (paid to the account) for board (food and lodging)		one year	13,,____,,____
1762_March 25th	To D (ditto)	for D (ditto)	one year	13,,____,,____
April 25th	To D (ditto)	for D (ditto)	one month	1,,__1,, 8
				+ £27,,__1,, 8

The male society in Williamsburg had questionable morals, and Thomas often referred to the college town as "Devilsburg." The young men liked cockfighting, gambling, drinking, racing, and wenching. Young Thomas sparingly participated in these activities. He never used tobacco, played cards, fought, and hardly drank, but did partake of the billiard table. He was more interested in courting the flirtatious belles, than the lesser temptations.

Thomas gave credit for his rescue from bad living to Dr. William Small, George Wythe, Esq., and his cousin Peyton Randolph, whom he held in high esteem and as a role model of integrity and judgment, and with whom he held long discussions about revolutionary politics. Although, Thomas was grateful to them for the huge influence that they had over his life as he grew into manhood, someone much earlier had made him feel that being "worthless to society" was a kind of sin. It was no doubt his father, whose giant shadow loomed behind him like the ghost of Hamlet's father.

Thomas began studying fifteen hours a day in the latter part of his college career. He read and studied by candlelight habitually until long past midnight, only to rise at dawn. Thomas would have profited from better illumination and better print, but even so, his eyes held out surprisingly well. His close college friend and cousin, John Page, reported that Thomas "...could tear himself away from his dearest friends, to fly to his studies."

> *I made a promise to Dr. Walker and myself that I would concentrate more on my studies. My only diversion was a swift and energizing one-mile evening run down Duke of Gloucester Street to a rock marker outside of Williamsburg, and then back, before returning to my books. I also made brisk walking a daily routine, for I believe that "the sovereign invigorator of the body is exercise, and of all of the exercises walking is the best."[19] My student life became a blend of physical and mental exercises. I remember how Father used to say, "A strong body makes the mind strong,"[20] and I have lived my life under that precept.*

Peter Jefferson's death left Thomas in the financial position of an independent country gentleman. While at college, Thomas had access to many bookshops. His early purchases included a Greek and Latin dictionary, poetry, law, and history books. He was happiest when he was around his books. The maturing young scholar became committed to his studies. He believed that all subjects were important and that reading good books was one of the best ways to employ, encourage, and direct the mind. He also became disappointed at the lack of interest that the other students showed in their studies, preferring gambling, smoking, and drinking over their education. Between the ages of 19 and 24, when most of Thomas's friends were engaged in other such activities, he largely buried himself with the kind of books that most of his friends avoided as difficult or esoteric.

> *The day's program of study that I followed my second year in college is similar to that which I follow to this day: Before 8 a.m. until twelve I read "... physical studies, Ethics, Religion, natural and sectarian, and natural law," and politics from twelve to one. In the afternoon, I occupy myself with history, and "from dark to bed-time," belles-lettres, rhetoric, and oratory.* [21]

Thomas Jefferson refers to "belles-lettres" in his program of study, as the art of writing. The most popular publications, and those he is known to have read, were written by Lord Chesterfield. "Rhetoric" is the ancient art of using language in order to persuade or influence others, and most likely a reference to the work of Cicero. For centuries, its study was regarded as a staple of a gentleman's education, being one of the seven 'liberal' arts, the other six being mathematics, grammar, logic, geometry, music and astronomy. "Oratory" is the art of public speaking, and in ancient times, was an important skill for any educated person who wanted to advance himself. Here, Thomas Jefferson is most likely referring to the work of Quintilian. Possessing rhetoric and oratory skills involves gestures to voice modulation, demanding the attention of one's mind in order to put together a solid argument, and necessary for political and legal advantage.

"It was my great good fortune, and what probably fixed the destinies of my life that Dr. Wm. Small of Scotland was then professor of Mathematics, a man profound in most of the useful branches of science, with a happy talent of communication, correct and gentlemanly manners, & an enlarged & liberal mind. He, most happily for me, became soon attached to me & made me his daily companion when not engaged in the school; and from his conversation I got my first views of the expansion of science & of the system of things in which we are placed." [22]

"To his enlightened and affectionate guidance of my studies while at college, I am indebted for everything...He first introduced into both schools rational and elevated courses of study, and, from an extraordinary conjunction of eloquence and logic, was enabled to communicate them to the students with great effect." [23]

Dr. William Small, a Scotsman educated at Marischal College at the University in Edinburgh, Scotland, galvanized the intellect of the young Thomas Jefferson. Dr. Small had been appointed professor of natural philosophy, mathematics, and science at The College of William & Mary in 1758. Soon after Thomas's arrival in 1760, Dr. Small also assumed the duties of teaching moral philosophy, introducing Thomas to the writings of Locke, Bacon, and Newton, and awakened an interest in science in the enthusiastic young student. For all practical purposes, Dr. Small was "the" college for Thomas Jefferson and was his only teacher during most of his time as a student. Unmarried and whose chief complaint was loneliness, Dr. Small made a daily companion of his favorite student, who found that Thomas had a thirst for learning equal to his own. A warm friendship sprang up between the two, despite the discrepancy of position and age, while Thomas developed an abiding love of science.

Dr. William Small
Courtesy of The Muscarelle Museum of Art
at The College of William & Mary in Virginia

Chapter XVIII:
Post-Graduate
Law Study

*I was nineteen when Dr. Small "...introduced me
to the acquaintance and familiar table of Governor
Fauquier, "the ablest man who ever filled that
office..., was musical also, being a good performer,
and associated me with two or three other amateurs
in his weekly concerts."*[24]

During Thomas' two years at The College of William
& Mary, Dr. Small had observed something in Thomas
worth cultivating, and introduced his new protégé to
Virginia's Lieutenant Governor Francis Fauquier and
to the brilliant lawyer, George Wythe. Thomas soon
attracted the attention of George Wythe, who proudly
enjoyed showing off the prize student to other men
who ruled Virginia.

By this time, it was the brilliance and open mind-
edness of the young Thomas Jefferson that inspired
Lieutenant Governor Fauquier to invite him to the
Governor's Palace, once a week for a fine dinner in the
state dining room, along with Dr. Small and George
Wythe. There he would spend hours after class involved
in stimulating conversation at the lieutenant governor's

hospitable and elegant mahogany dinner table with the elite group. The topics ranged over many subjects, including science, religion, and philosophy, where no doubt Jefferson heard unfamiliar points of view, and so enlarged his mind. Thomas was often invited to play in the Palace ballroom with a small amateur chamber group that the lieutenant governor had established.

The Governor's Palace, residence of the king's deputy
The Colonial Williamsburg Foundation

With him, and at his table, Dr. Small & Mr. Wythe, his amici omnium horarum, & myself, formed a partie quarrée, & to the habitual conversations on these occasions I owe much instruction."[25] It was "at these dinners I have heard more good sense, more rational and philosophical conversation than in all my life besides.*[26]

Dr. Small, Lieutenant Governor Fauquier, and Mr. Wythe, the "amici omnium horarum," (translated "friends of all hours", as Thomas referred to them) habitually made Thomas the fourth member of their circle, the "partie quarrée" or "foursome." From Dr. Small, he gained a conception of the scope of philosophy. From George Wythe, one of the foremost classical scholars in the colonies, he learned great principles of politics. And from Lieutenant Governor Fauquier, he acquired the refinements of society and music. But, more importantly, the young man from the tiny county of Albemarle was exposed to the thoughts current in Europe, commonly referred to as the Enlightenment. He was introduced to theater, politics, and to culture that he never knew existed.

Thomas Jefferson graduated with supreme honors from The College of William & Mary on April 25, 1762, having completed all his studies in two years. Upon graduation, Thomas possessed great acumen and was well versed in the knowledge of Greek and Latin, as well as in history, philosophy, literature, art, and architecture... all hallmarks of education for an eighteenth-century gentleman.

> *Upon my graduation from William & Mary, I was invited to study at the law office and home of my distinguished friend, George Wythe. Most students generally studied law for two years, but I happily accepted his offer and continued for the next five years reading and studying law under Mr. Wythe's tutelage. While in Williamsburg, I boarded at the Market Square Tavern on Duke of Gloucester Street,*

which was owned by Mr. Thomas Craig and his wife, who also operated a tavern and a tailor shop.

Market Square Tavern
The Colonial Williamsburg Foundation

During the week, I would walk to Mr. Wythe's house, enter through the back door, and proceed to Mr. Wythe's study on the right, where he would be waiting for me. In the student's room, I studied mathematics, natural philosophy and the classics as well as law. Among the classical writers, I read Homer, Euripides, Virgil, Seneca, Cicero, Milton, Shakespeare, and John Locke. I began the study of law by reading the Englishman's introductory law book, Coke Upon Littleton, the dense prose by Sir Edward Coke. I also studied the English statutes from the Magna Carta to the time of James I, criminal law, and the treatise on jurisdiction. An abridgement of the Acts of Assembly for Virginia, up to January 1, 1758, was also available to me.

Wythe House Rear Entrance
The Colonial Williamsburg Foundation

When Thomas was just beginning his required reading assignment, he wrote to John Page, "Well, Page,
I do wish the Devil had old Cooke (Coke), for I am
sure I never was so tired on an old dull scoundrel in
my life." [27] But, Thomas had gone on to conquer Coke,
and in time, came to admire his "uncouth but cunning
learning."[28]

George Wythe was born in 1726 on his family's
plantation on the Back River in Elizabeth City County,
Virginia. After finishing his course of study at The
College of William & Mary, he studied law, was admitted to the bar at the age of twenty, and rose rapidly in
his profession. He and his wife, Elizabeth Taliaferro,
lived in the house that Elizabeth's father, an architect, designed and built for them on the Palace Green,
known today as the Wythe House.

George Wythe, Esquire
The Colonial Williamsburg Foundation

George Wythe was the dean of law at The College of William & Mary, the first professor of law in America at the college, and an elected burgess representing The College of William & Mary. He had a reputation for having great legal skill and integrity, who taught natural philosophy, emphasizing to his law students the importance of observation and using reason to solve a problem, as well as to consider how laws would impact others. He was said to be one of the finest lawyers of that day. Occasionally, he took on young men for private instruction, and as a result of Dr. Small's influence, Thomas would be one such student. George Wythe's students would consult with him at his home office and then be advised of their reading assignments. The students were required to listen at the door of the lobby of the House of Burgesses whenever meetings were in session.

> *On Saturday's, the other law students and I would argue fake cases in moot court in the Capitol Building General Court Room, a law school activity and competition where we prepared and argued the case in front of judges. Each case and side was selected beforehand, and we were given a set amount of time to prepare for the eventual trial. I will never forget losing my first case to none other than Patrick Henry… to my dismay, a self-taught lawyer.*
>
> *After a long week, my friends and I looked forward to Saturday evenings, and together would meet for dinner, then either attend a play, a dance, or concert. On Sundays, I attended service at Bruton Church with Dabney, then afterward read and prepared for the upcoming week.*

General Court Room, Capitol Building
The Colonial Williamsburg Foundation

The General Court, the highest judicial tribunal in the colony, met twice yearly here in the Capitol. Civil cases occupied most of its attention, but criminal offenses punishable by death also came before it.

> *Mr. Wythe was in favor of and recommended that I continue the lifelong practice of keeping a Commonplace Book to journal my thoughts, document observations, and record all business transactions and financial accounts…a practice I have embraced to this day.* "Mr. Wythe continued to be my faithful and beloved Mentor in youth, and my most affectionate friend through life." "He was my ancient master, my earliest and best friend, and to him I am indebted for first impressions which have had the most salutary influence on the course of my life."[29]

In total, Thomas devoted five years to studying law under George Wythe. After some time living in Williamsburg and reading with George Wythe as his apprentice, Thomas left Williamsburg for Shadwell to continue his studies. Learning law in Virginia at that time, was not as well structured as it was in England, but it was the most common form of learning law in a land where there were no law schools established. Jefferson, though, was very adept at learning the law profession from books, rather than from practice.

> *While studying under Mr. Wythe's tutelage, I remember my first organized effort was to improve the navigation on the Rivanna. Flooding had been one of father's greatest concerns… one shared by other mill owners, as well as those that navigated*

the river. Unpredictable weather and the forces of nature always had the final say, and making the Rivanna safer to navigate was an ongoing issue for those of us in the plantation industry. As it turned out, the mill that father built shortly before his death in 1757 operated until May of 1771, when the great fresh destroyed it. I plan to rebuild a manufacturing mill on the Rivanna, but feel that another dam is necessary upstream to help control the water flow.

Thomas Jefferson did rebuild a new manufacturing mill on the Rivanna, as well as build another dam approximately one-fourth of a mile upstream from the site of his father's dam. Today, the ruins of Thomas Jefferson's four-story manufacturing mill, completed in 1803, are still visible on the north bank of the river three-fourths of a mile past his dam.

The word "fresh," referred to as the "great fresh," is most commonly used to describe a spring thaw resulting from snow and ice melting where the rivers freeze each winter and thaw during the spring. A spring "fresh" can sometimes last several weeks on large river systems, resulting in significant inundation of flood plains in the rivers' watershed. Spring fresh associated with the thaw events are sometimes accompanied by ice jams, which can cause flash floods. These major ice jams develop during the spring fresh when the rising water levels start to break up the previously stable ice cover.

Chapter XIX: From Boy to Man

While studying law in Williamsburg, Thomas experienced an early disappointment in love when he attempted to court a highly sought-after and beautiful, but pious, young lady named Rebecca Lewis Burwell, of Fairfield, the great-granddaughter of Robert "King" Carter of Shirley plantation in Charles City County. Rebecca's mother, Mary Willis, died giving birth to her on May 26, 1746, and her father, British Naval Colonel Lewis Burwell III, died when she was ten, leaving Rebecca and her older brother, Lewis, orphaned. Once orphaned, Lewis and Rebecca were raised in Yorktown at the home of their father's sister, Elizabeth, and her gentry husband William Nelson.

In the mid-1730s, Rebecca's father, Colonel Lewis Burwell III, established a 1,400-acre plantation which he named Fairfield, in Gloucester County. It included a mansion, outbuildings and a garden. Colonel Burwell was the colonial customs inspector for the upper James River, calling the site of his inspection station Burwell's Landing. The property featured a tavern, storehouse, warehouse, and ferry house.

Rebecca was the object of Thomas Jefferson's first adolescent crush, as he often referred to her as his "fair

Belinda." In his many references of her, Thomas often disguised Rebecca's name by giving her nicknames such as Belinda, Becca, Adneleb (Belenda backward), and even wrote her name in Greek as "αδνιλεβ." It is very possible that he drew her nickname from Alexander Pope's mock-heroic narrative poem *The Rape of the Lock*, originally found in a book of prose in Peter Jefferson's Shadwell library. The poem satirizes the main character, Petre, who while lusting after Belinda, cuts off a lock of her hair without her permission. Consequently, an argument ensues, creating a rift between the two families in the story.

In 1762, Thomas met the nearly sixteen-year-old Rebecca while she was in Williamsburg attending the wedding of her brother, Lewis. Not only was Thomas a classmate of Lewis Burwell at The College of William & Mary, but Thomas's cousin, Judith Page, was to marry him. It was on the day of the wedding that Thomas met Rebecca Burwell, and from that day forward, was totally smitten.

Coincidentally, Lewis Burwell's tuition entry is right above Thomas' in the Bursar Records, which means that they registered for classes at the same time. (See Tuition Entry image in Chapter XVII)

Shortly after, Rebecca had given Thomas a silhouette of her profile, and he affixed the cutout to the back of his watch case. Thomas was miserable when he found that a leaking roof dripped water on to his watch, and in his endeavor to remove the soaked silhouette, as he describes in a letter to John Page in Williamsburg dated Christmas day, 1762, "My cursed fingers gave them such a rent as I fear I never shall get over." The "dear picture" was hopelessly torn. "And now although the picture be defaced … there is so lively an image of her imprinted in my mind that I shall think of her too often. I fear for my peace of mind, and too often I am sure to get through Old Cooke (Coke) this winter: for God knows I have not seen him since I packed him up in my trunk in Williamsburg."[30]

Thomas decided to spend the early winter months of 1763 at Shadwell, instead of returning back to Williamsburg. While at home, he studied the writings of Sir Edward Coke, which as a law student he was expected to do, but, unfortunately, came down with an eye infection which kept him from being able to read.

The following quote from a letter to John Page is strong evidence of his restlessness. He wrote, "All things here appear to me to trudge on in one and the same round…. We rise in the morning that we may eat breakfast, dinner, and supper and go to bed again that we may get up the next morning and do the same. Had I better stay here and do nothing, or go down and do less? …Inclination tells me to go, receive my sentence, and be no longer in suspense; but, reason says if you go and your attempt proves unsuccessful you will be ten times more wretched than ever."[31]

> *At 19, after returning home to Shadwell for winter break, I endeavored to build a flatboat suitable for sailing the Rivanna, and fantasized sailing it to "England Holland France Spain and Italy (where I would buy me a good fiddle) and Egypt and return through the British provinces to the north-*

ward home."[32] The project kept me from thinking about the young lady that I longed for, and the friends that I missed during the long, cold winter.

Thomas urged John Page, in a letter, to sail with him to England and the Mediterranean in the flatboat that he was building, which he named "Rebecca." He writes, "This, to be sure, would take us two to three years and if we should not both be cured of love in that time I think the devil would be in it." Thomas kept the letter at his home in Shadwell for two months before sending it, adding even more melancholy and dramatic postscripts, "I verily believe Page that I shall die soon, and yet I can give no other reason for it but that I am tired with living. At this moment when I am writing I am scarcely sensible that I exist."[33]

John Page warned Thomas, apparently what he already knew, that there was a rival in Rebecca's life, and urged Thomas "to go immediately and lay siege in form." But Thomas continued to sulk at home in Shadwell, staying there nine months, from early January to early October 1763, despite the fact that he was supposed to be studying law with George Wythe in Williamsburg.

Thomas begged John Page to intercede on his behalf to Rebecca, explaining to her why he must visit England before approaching her uncle about the possibility of marriage. Thomas wrote, "I should be scared to death at making so unreasonable a proposal as that of waiting until I returned from Britain, unless she could be first prepared for it."[34] Whether Thomas's mother was discouraging the courtship, and using the trip to

England to visit relatives as a device to keep him under watch, we do not know. Thomas continued to relay his feelings about Rebecca in excerpts from the same letter,

> Shadwell, July 15th 1763
>
> Dear Page,
>
> …The rival you mentioned I know not whether to think formidable or not as there has been so great an opening for him during my absence. …You advise me to 'go immediately and lay siege in form. … If I am to succeed the sooner I know it the less uneasiness I shall have to go through: if I am to meet with a disappointment the sooner I know it the more of life I shall have of life to wear it off: an if I do meet with one, I hope in god and verily believe it will be the last. …and if Belinda will not accept of my service it shall never be offered to another. … Make my compliments to her…
>
> > I am, Dear Page, Your sincere friend,
> > T. Jefferson[35]

After isolating himself at Shadwell for nine months, Thomas returned to Williamsburg. On the evening of October 6, 1763, while Rebecca was visiting her brother, Lewis, and his wife, Judith, in Gloucester County outside of Williamsburg, she attended a ball held at the Apollo in the Raleigh Tavern on Gloucester Street. It was common for a gentleman and a lady to frequent such an event, and to openly mingle and dance with everyone who was in attendance. On this particular evening, Thomas gathered up his courage to approach Rebecca to ask her to wait for him while he went to England, making a clumsy marriage proposal. The request proved unattractive to Rebecca, and she rejected his proposal. Stammering slightly with nerves, he attempted again. The final conversation apparently ended his advances, if not his infatuation.

As he described it in a letter to his friend John Page, Thomas made something of a fool of himself. Obviously, he was not as prolific with the tongue, as he was with the quill. He wrote…

Williamsburg, October 7, 1763

Dear Page,

…In the most melancholy fit that ever any poor soul was, I sit down to write to you. Last night, as merry as agreeable company and dancing with Belinda in the Apollo could make me, I never could have thought the succeeding sun would have seen me so wretched as I now am. I was prepared to say a great deal. I had dressed up in my own mind such thoughts as occurred to me, in as moving language as I know how, and expected to have performed in a tolerably creditable manner. But, good God! When I had an opportunity of venting them, a few broken sentences, uttered in great disorder, and interrupted with pauses of uncommon length, were the too visible marks of my strange confusion! …

I am, dear Page, your sincere friend,
T. Jefferson[36]

Though John Page had urged him to make another visit to her, Thomas refused, and indicated that he had then lost all hope, "A visit could not possibly be of the least weight."[37]

During his Christmas vacation in 1764, Thomas and John Page wrote to each other more about Rebecca and John's love, Nancy Wilson, than about their studies. Thomas feared that the letters they had written to each other, would become "the subjects of a great deal of mirth and raillery" if gotten into the wrong hands. He continued, "We must fall on some scheme of communicating our thoughts to each other, which shall be totally unintelligible to everyone but to ourselves."[38]

Resigned to being turned down by Rebecca, Thomas dropped his pursuit, stopped talking of going to England, and plunged deeper into his law studies. A few months later, Rebecca's neighbor and childhood friend, Jacqueline Ambler, requested her hand in marriage. News of Rebecca's engagement and pending marriage triggered the first of many severe headaches that would sporadically plague him.

At eleven o'clock at night, on March 20, 1764, racked by a violent headache in which he had suffered for two days, Thomas wrote to his friend William Fleming regarding the finality of the lost relationship, "With regard to the scheme which I proposed to you some time since, I am sorry to tell you it is totally frustrated by Miss R.B.'s marriage with Jacqueline Ambler which the people here tell me they daily expect...Well the Lord bless her I say!"[39] Rebecca and Jacqueline Ambler married on May 24, 1764.

Chapter XX: Peter Jefferson's Legacy

As a boy, I learned about nature and many practical skills from father, while accompanying him around the farm, such as about insects, flowers, seasonal plants, vegetables, and fruits. Father showed me how to use a gun, hunt, fish, paddle a canoe, plow, shoe a horse, and to know the forest as few other boys did. I will never forget the day he gave me a gun and sent me into the forest, alone, in order to develop my self-reliance. I was ten years old, but I persevered. I remember finding a wild turkey caught in a pen. I carefully retrieved it, "tied it with my garter to a tree, shot it, and brought it home to father in triumph."[40] Hunting through the Southwest Mountains near Shadwell had then become a favorite pastime of mine and later, an admirable form of exercise.

Peter's Mountain, taken from Turkey Sag Road
Southwest Mountain Range, Albemarle County, Virginia
Author's personal photo library

Father showed me how to use the mathematical instruments in his surveyor's kit, such as the iron measuring chains, steel-tipped pens, and the brass-bound compass, explaining how they were used to measure the contour of large tracts of land. I always enjoyed listening to his frontier stories when visitors came to Shadwell, and will forever cherish my memories spent with him.

The measuring chain used by Peter Jefferson was invented in 1620 by Englishman, Edmund Gunter. It was made of 100 iron or steel links and was 66 feet long. Eighty chains made up one mile. Ten square chains made one acre. Gunter's chain was in universal use until the steel tape measure replaced it in the last decades of the eighteenth century. The brassbound compass, invented in 1511, was in wide use until 1894.

Early surveys were often grossly inaccurate, since the iron chains stretched with use. The magnetic compass was a major source of error. It was subject to daily, annual, and lunar variations in the earth's magnetic field, solar magnetic storms, local attractions and static electricity in the compass glass. Optical glass also varied in quality. There were no standards for equipment, and there was no way to recalibrate equipment damaged one hundred miles from civilization. Survey procedures were often less than precise. If a tree blocked a line of sight, a surveyor might sight to the trunk, walk around it and approximate the continuing line. Precision seemed unimportant to the early surveyors, since the land seemed endless and, at $1.25 an acre, cheap, especially to a surveyor who was paid by the mile. Other factors contributing to inaccuracy included a lack of supervision, a shortage of trained surveyors, an abundance of hostile Indians, bears, wolves, wind, rain, snow, burning sun and rugged terrain.

Peter Jefferson was considered an accomplished man of his day, and a pillar of his community. He was a surveyor, a member of the House of Burgesses, a county justice, and served as sheriff of Albemarle County. He was judge of the Court of Chancery, commissioned as lieutenant colonel in the Albemarle County militia, a vestryman at St. James, Northam Parish, and a devoted husband and father. Peter Jefferson was a successful planter, and the owner of more than sixty slaves, along with twenty-five horses, seventy head of cattle, and two hundred hogs. He was industrious, fiercely independent, and a self-made man.

Before he died, Peter amassed approximately 7,500 acres, most being in Albemarle County, of which Thomas would inherit 2,650 acres upon his twenty-first birthday. Besides acquiring large tracts of land, Peter led numerous surveying expeditions, surveyed tens of thousands of acres of frontier wilderness, and created some of the most detailed and accurate maps of his day.

Upon his death, Peter Jefferson left his sons the Shadwell plantation on the Rivanna and the Snowden plantation on the Fluvanna, allowing his eldest son, Thomas, to choose between the two properties. Thomas chose Shadwell, leaving Snowden to his younger brother, Randolph.

Until I turned 21, I had no part in the supervision of father's estate. On April 13, 1764, I immediately declared my financial independence, assuming my rightful place as head of the family, and was then able to divide up the estate with Randolph, who was nine years old at the time. Being the oldest, I received my portion of the slaves, as well as my preferred choice of father's land holdings. I chose the 2,750 acres along the Rivanna; which included Shadwell, Pantops, and Pouncey's in Fredericksville Parish, Tufton, Portobello in St. Anne's Parish, and the acreage I later named Monticello. I began the active management of the Shadwell plantation, which produced tobacco as its main cash crop. Father bequeathed to me some 42 books, which included his account books as Albemarle Surveyor, his cherry-tree desk and bookcases, maps, and his mathematical instruments and surveying journals that he used during his surveying days.

When my dear brother Randolph came of age, he inherited the remaining portion of the Fluvanna lands, some 2,292 acres in Buckingham County, along with the 1,300 acre Snowden plantation, and a similar portion of slaves and livestock. Located 16 miles south of Shadwell, father named the Snowden acreage after a beautiful mountain in Wayles. The land is situated on the south side of Horseshoe Bend, overlooking the town of Scott's Landing on the Fluvanna River.

The Snowden property is located on a peninsula-type landform that was uniquely forged by geologic processes over the course of time. The land's horseshoe shape is what gave the bend in the river its name.

Horseshoe Bend is an isolated meander of the Fluvanna River, and is bound to the east and west by long, relatively straight stretches of river.

Snowden Property at Horseshoe Bend
on James River, Virginia
Burgess Collection, The Scottsville
Museum, Scottsville, Virginia

In colonial times, the colonists called the stretch of the James River that flowed east through the county of Fluvanna, the Fluvanna River. The river name changed back to James River at the port town of Columbia, four kilometers (two and a half miles) east of Scott's Landing. Today, the entire stretch of river is only referred to as the James River, which flows through the Shenandoah Valley and the Blue Ridge Mountains in a southeastern direction. After leaving the Blue Ridge, the river turns to the northeast at Lynchburg, then just west of Scott's Landing, the river turns southeast again.

The Native Indians, and later the English colonists prospecting for land to establish their plantations, were first attracted to the area because of its highly fertile soil along the river, and its natural ford. A natural ford in a river tends to slow the current, making it easier to cross. Edward Scott, one such land prospector in 1732, patented 550 acres of land on the northwest curve of the river's horseshoe shaped bend, and called it Scott's Landing. Due to its fertile lowlands along the river, and the land tracts' proximity to the river, the area became a bustling port and major thoroughfare for trade and transportation during colonial times, and played a central role in the region's development.

After the county of Albemarle was established in September 1744 by an Act of the Virginia Assembly, to become effective on January 1, 1745, the area settlers selected Scott's Landing as Albemarle's first county seat due to its position on the river and north-south trade route. The magistrates commissioned Edward Scott's son, Daniel, to build a ferry at Scott's Landing to serve as a local ferry crossing for inhabitants living and trading on both sides of the Fluvanna River, as well as a river port for the batteau transportation down the James River. Edward Scott's house, Totier (identified today as Valmont or Bell Grove), located on the south side of the river, was then easily accessible by Scott's Ferry, and served as the county's meeting place.

On February 26, 1745, the first five justices were sworn in for the newly formed Albemarle County and the town of Scott's Landing. The following June, the County Commissioners authorized the construction of a courthouse, prison, stocks, and pillory on the south side of the Fluvanna. All roads seemed to lead to Scott's Landing, until 1762 when the county seat was moved north to the small town of Charlottesville on the Rivanna River, named in honor of Princess Charlotte, who became queen of England after marrying King George III in 1761.

Portraits of King George III and Queen Charlotte
by Studio of Allan Ramsay, London, England, circa 1770
The Colonial Williamsburg Foundation. Museum Purchase.

In the new town of Charlottesville, the northern street was named Jefferson Street, the southern street was named South Street, and the intervening east-west streets were Market and Main. The two-acre public square on the north side of Jefferson Street, the site for the county courthouse and jail, remained county property, as it still is today. The cross streets were Court (now 5th Street), Union (now 1st Street), and Hill (now 2nd Street West). A frame courthouse, pillory, stocks, and whipping post were all erected in the public square soon after 1761.

However, the move of the county seat from Scott's Landing to Charlottesville, coupled with the formation of a new county and change in the county lines, negatively impacted the influence and prestige of Scott's Landing. But, the town remained an important port, and tobacco inspection station, as a result of its location on the natural ford, and therefore remained ideal for shipping.

Scott's Ferry operated over the James River at Scottsville for 162 years before being replaced in 1907 by the first bridge. After many years of useful service, the wood-planked bridge was replaced in 1968 by the concrete bridge in use today. (Visit smuseum@avenue. org)

The original Snowden home, built on a bluff by Peter Jefferson, was later occupied by his youngest son, Randolph Jefferson, and his family, until Randolph's death on August 7, 1815. The original home accidentally burned to the ground circa 1857, and a similar home was built to replace it by the succeeding owner. At the time that the Jefferson's owned the property, the only way to cross was by the Scott's Landing ferry.

Snowden House, built circa1857, Scott's Landing, Virginia
Burgess Collection, The Scottsville
Museum, Scottsville, Virginia

*To my six sisters, father allotted a slave and £200
each, which was to be paid within a year of their
marriage or upon their 21st birthday. Seventeen
year old Jane chose Patt, although at first, Jane did
not want a slave assigned to her. Sixteen year old
Mary wanted Nan. Thirteen year old Elizabeth
inherited Cate. Eleven year old Martha inherited
Rachel. Five year old Lucy inherited Cachina and
her children, Phebe and Lydia. Two year old Anna
Scott inherited Eve, and Randolph inherited Peter.*

*I inherited father's personal man servant,
Sawney, who was much older than I. Sawney was
a trained shoemaker at Shadwell, and responsible
for guiding and teaching me personal grooming,
commonly referring to me as "master."*

The Jefferson children saw their parents show kindness to the slaves, but they also grew up with the understanding that they were the bosses of their assigned slaves. Sometime after Peter Jefferson's death, and before Thomas left to attend The College of William & Mary, Sawney died, and Thomas replaced him with his nineteen-year-old childhood slave friend, Jupiter, who was born at Shadwell plantation in 1743, the same year as Thomas. Jupiter worked in the barn with the horses, as well as the lumber mill. He was bright and took pride in his daily responsibilities. Thomas observed his value as being more than just a farm hand, and for fifty years of their lives, they were bound together by law, as well as friendship.

> *"When the famous Resolutions of 1765 against the Stamp-act were proposed, I was yet a student of law in Williamsburg."* The next day, *"I attended the debate, however, at the door of the lobby of the House of Burgesses, and heard the splendid display of Mr. Henry's talents as a popular orator. They were great indeed; such as I have never heard from any other man."*[41]
>
> *Patrick Henry had, just the year before, been elected to the House of Burgesses, and shortly after, became the leading radical member of the aristocratic group of legislators. My cousin Peyton Randolph was standing next to me, witnessing the unforgettable speech, as Henry tried in vain to encourage the passage of the resolutions, arguing defiantly against Great Britain.*
>
> *Although I was inclined to look down upon Henry as an uncouth and uneducated backwoods-*

man, I had to admit that on this occasion, he was a splendid orator. "He appeared to me to speak as Homer wrote," [42] with "torrents of sublime eloquence." [43]

In 1765 the British Parliament passed the Stamp Act, which placed a tax on newspapers, almanacs, pamphlets, all kinds of legal documents, insurance policies, ship's papers, licenses, dice and playing cards. It had been passed by the British Parliament to help pay off some of its debt from its various wars, including the French and Indian War fought in part to protect the colonies. This led to widespread protest throughout the colonies, as they chanted the slogan, "No taxation without representation!"

The Virginia Resolves, or Resolutions of 1765, issued on May 29th, were a series of resolutions passed by the Virginia House of Burgesses in response to the Stamp Act. The resolves claimed that in accordance with long established British law, Virginia was subject to taxation only by a parliamentary assembly to which Virginians themselves elected representatives. Since no colonial representatives were elected to the Parliament, the only assembly legally allowed to raise taxes would be the Virginia General Assembly, not Parliament. Hence a rift began.

Chapter XXI:
Jane, Farewell
Forever and Ever

On October 1, 1765, my beloved sister, Jane, died. Sadly, she was only 25 years old… too young for such a vibrant woman in the prime of her life. I was home for a short vacation from studying law in Williamsburg, when Jane suddenly died. It has been 9 years, and I still cannot bring myself to even write about that awful day.

Devastated by her passing, I fell into a period of deep mourning. Throughout our lives, Jane took such delight in being my older sister, and I enjoyed the attention. She was always a great source of encouragement, a trusted confidant, and my constant companion growing up. We shared a deep friendship, and held no secrets between each other. I feel safe in believing that Jane knew me better than any other person in my life.

When in church, I can still recall the sweet sound of Jane singing her favorite hymn while standing next to me, Love Divine, All Loves Excelling … a melody so familiar to me since my youth. We were truly kindred spirits, and I will forever grieve her passing.

> *I still struggle with loneliness, and have noticed that since her death, I have become more reclusive. Often times, I find solace walking along the river or riding along the tobacco field where we spent most of our childhood. Reading my books, writing in my notebook, or meditating in prayer seems to be my only solace.*
>
> *The epitaph that I dedicated to her was written by the poet William Shenstone, which read, "Jane Jefferson, Ah, Joanna, best of girls. Ah, torn away from the bloom of vigorous age. May the earth be light upon you. Farewell, forever and ever."*[44]

Only Thomas's mother and younger siblings, Elizabeth, Lucy, and the twins Anna Scott and Randolph, were living at home after Jane's death. Thomas drew little comfort from his younger siblings, as they did not provide him with the same intellectual stimulation as the older sisters, Jane and Mary, had. Elizabeth was only one year younger, but was mentally deficient. Lucy was only thirteen years old, and the twins were just ten.

Ill health had prevented Thomas from embarking on a long-planned trip to Europe, which had been arranged in view of his then limited exposure to the world outside of Virginia. He settled for a brief tour of the middle Atlantic colonies in May of 1765, which included stays in Annapolis, Philadelphia, and New York. These travels were able to distract Thomas from his disappointments with Rebecca Burwell and the recent death of his beloved sister.

While in Philadelphia, Thomas, then twenty-three, underwent the smallpox inoculation, which was progressive thinking at the time, even though the inoculation was widely discouraged. Smallpox was one of the most feared diseases in the eighteenth century. A high percentage of those infected died, and many who survived were blinded or badly disfigured.

Inoculation against smallpox had been introduced into Europe from the Middle East early in the century and subsequently conveyed to the American colonies, but it was not without risk. There were deaths associated with the inoculation process, as it introduced the disease into the system in a milder form. There was also the real concern that smallpox could be spread through an inoculated person who was not properly quarantined. Therefore, the inoculation often encountered fear and much opposition.

Chapter XXII:
Lawyer, Vestryman, Politician, Planter

By the age of twenty-four, Thomas had gained quite an education beyond the provincial book learning. He observed a session in the Maryland state legislature, and generally rubbed elbows with people of various backgrounds and origins. He established many important contacts in his travels, as well as through his affiliation with the distinguished George Wythe. Thomas concluded his law studies in Williamsburg, received his law degree, was admitted to the Virginia Bar on February 12, 1767, and entered, at once, the practice of law before the General Court in Charlottesville.

At that time, the village of Charlottesville contained little besides a dozen houses, the general courthouse, and the Swan Tavern, where the Red-Land Club now stands. The original courthouse structure was replaced in 1803 by a rectangular brick courthouse, or north portion of the present-day building. This building was the public building of the town of Charlottesville, which Thomas Jefferson referred to as "the common temple."[45] It was used for sittings of the magistrates' courts, for public assemblies, for church services by different denominations, and as the main precinct for local elections. Here Thomas Jefferson visited frequently, as a lawyer, magistrate, church attendant, voter, and an attendee to various local meetings.

General Courthouse, Charlottesville, Virginia
Author's personal photo library

Upon concluding my studies under George Wythe and passing the bar exam in February 1767, I left Williamsburg to oversee the mismanaged mill at Shadwell, and provide stability for my siblings. With a cartful of books and all my belongings, I returned to Shadwell and assumed total control of the family plantation, paying close attention to all activities and expenses at Shadwell, as well as help my sisters tend to mother's garden.

On the 12th of February, I took on my first case, and thereafter, continued to work before the

General Court in the village of Charlottesville, initiated a successful law practice, and won established clients all across Virginia. My first year in practice, I handled 68 cases, which grew to 115 cases the second year, and 198 the third year.

On August 23, 1767, I traveled to the town of Staunton, in Augusta County, to perform legal services regarding several cases. After leaving Staunton, and on my way to Bedford, I came across "the most sublime of Nature's works."[46] I paid a local man to guide me to the magnificent structure up close. Once we arrived, I took out my Memorandum Book, and on the inside back cover, wrote the description of what seemed to be a natural bridge made from one rock of limestone, and I sketched it.

A small creek, called Cedar Creek, runs underneath the bridge, "being very rocky it is not rapid." "It is impossible for the emotions, arising from the sublime, to be felt beyond what they are...so beautiful an arch, so elevated, so light, and springing, as it were, up to heaven, the rapture of the spectator is really indescribable!"[47]

After completing legal business at the Amherst, Orange, Culpeper, Frederick and Fauquier County seats, I returned to Monticello and began to take steps to purchase the property surrounding what I call, Natural Bridge. I purchased the land from King George III for 20 shillings, and have recently received the patent for the 157-acre tract which includes the geological marvel. At some point, I hope to build a log cabin there and use it as a retreat.

Natural Bridge, Natural Bridge, Virginia
The Colonial Williamsburg Foundation

When Thomas Jefferson first saw the limestone bridge on August 23, 1767, he took notes on the inside back cover of his *Memorandum Book*. He later recorded his notes about the bridge in his *Notes on the State of Virginia*, where he wrote,

> "The Natural Bridge, the most sublime of nature's works...the fissure, just at the bridge, is, by some admeasurements, 270 feet deep, by others only 205. It is about forty-five feet wide

at the bottom, and ninety feet at the top; this of course determines the length of the bridge, and its height from the water. Its breadth in the middle is about sixty feet, but more at the ends, and the thickness of the mass at the summit of the arch, about forty feet. A part of this thickness is constituted by a coat of earth, which gives growth to many large trees. The residue, with the hill on both sides, is one solid rock of limestone... Though the sides of this bridge are provided in some parts with a parapet of fixed rocks, yet few men have resolution to walk to them, and look over into the abyss. You involuntarily fall on your hands and feet, creep to the parapet, and peep over it. Looking down from this height about a minute gave me a violent headache. If the view from the top is painful and intolerable, that from below is delightful in an equal extreme..."

On June 10, 1773, Jefferson paid the secretary of the colony at the surveyor general's office for a survey warrant and recorded it in his Memorandum Book:

"Pd. at S.O. returng. my own 157 as. for Natural Bridge. £2-15s-4d." (2 pounds of gold-15 shillings of silver-4denarius of copper) Shortly thereafter Jefferson paid James Tremble £2-1s-8d (2pounds of gold-1shilling of silver-8denarius of copper) "for making survey of my entry on Natural Bridge."

On July 5, 1774, a patent in the name of George III was issued to him.

The monetary exchange was as follows: £1(pound of gold) = 20s (shillings of silver), and 6s (shillings of silver) = $1 (Spanish dollar). Thus £2-15s-4d equals about 55s, or $9 (Spanish dollars), and £2-1s-8d=41s, or $7 (Spanish dollars). The grand total for the purchase is 96s, or $16 (Spanish dollars), roughly $160 using today's currency, in 1773.

Jefferson often thought of building a small hermitage where he might spend part of every year. He attempted, unsuccessfully, to sell the property in 1809, and instead leased it for saltpeter mining and for use as a shot tower. Several years later, he wrote in a letter to William Carmichael, dated December 26, 1786, stating that he had no intention of selling the land, and that he viewed it as a public trust, and would not permit the bridge to be injured, defaced, or masked from the public.

Thomas Jefferson eventually built a two-room log cabin, with one room reserved for guests. While President, in 1802, he surveyed the area with his own hands. In awe, famous people painted it and wrote about it. Thousands came by horse, stagecoach, and eventually train to view the huge, mysterious, renowned rock bridge. (See Appendix VI.)

When my executor, John Harvie, resigned as a vestryman of the Middle Church in Fredericksville Parish, I was asked to replace him. Father had held this position when he was alive, as well as justice of the peace, which duties I was asked to also perform. Unfortunately, I was only able to serve on the vestry for three years, due to my involvement with the family businesses, my call to local politics, and the design and preparation of my hilltop dwelling at Monticello.

Well after Thomas Jefferson's death, members of the Middle Church vestry decided that the church building was no longer adequate, and desired to update and improve the existing structure. In 1845, a committee enlisted the services of the wealthy colonial tobacco planter nationally famous architect, William Strickland, to head the project. William Strickland chose Gothic Revival as the style, which was considered an expression of wealth and class distinction. It was the desire that the church be an outstanding architectural, artistic, and religious achievement that would long endure. Construction began in 1846 and the church renovation was completed in 1854. Unfortunately, William Strickland died on April 6, 1854, a year before the church was completed on May 9, 1855.

Forty years later, in 1895, a fire destroyed what had been renamed Grace Church, leaving only the bell tower and four walls standing. The 1,575-pound bell was salvaged from the ashes and is still in use today. Grace Church was rebuilt in 1896, and still claims to be one of the six churches in the state of Virginia that has remained an active congregation since colonial times. Foundation stones from the original wood structure of 1748 are still visible today under the spreading oak trees in front of the historic church.

Grace Episcopal Church, Walker's Parish
Author's personal photo library
Courtesy of Grace Episcopal Church Vestry,
Jefferson Highway, Cismont, Virginia

My dear friend, Lieutenant Governor Fauquier, who was recuperating from a severe illness, retired as lieutenant governor in Williamsburg, and, sadly, he died shortly afterward. His successor, Governor Norborne Botetourt succeeded him on December 9, 1768, and as was customary, the Virginia Assembly was dissolved. "In 1769, I became a member of the legislature by the choice of the county in which I live"[48] and served as the Albemarle County delegate in the House of Burgesses, where I currently sit, thus becoming an integral part of the colonial law making body. "I made one effort in that body for the permission of the emancipation of slaves, which was rejected."[49]

Besides being an active vestryman, Thomas Jefferson was an accurate, painstaking, and laborious lawyer, and as a result, his business blossomed into a surprisingly large practice. As a vestry member, he and the other members were responsible for the selection of a minister when the need arose, care for the parish's poor and mentally deficient, setting of land boundaries, and requiring residents of the parish to pay a levy of tobacco or cash to support the church.

In the seven and a half years that he practiced law, Thomas Jefferson handled more than 940 cases. His specialty was the caveat, a touchy branch of land patent litigation, although he interested himself in the spicy divorce case, *Blair* vs. *Blair*. He pleaded for inoculation suit defendants, and took "*pro bono*" a hopeless case for the manumission of mulatto slave Samuel Howell, in Howell vs. Netherland, April 1770.

> *Generally speaking, I was a reasonably successful lawyer, although I often did not press many of my clients for payment. The main source of my income, and that of my family's, has always been from our plantations, as well as the income received from various real estate endeavors to improve the personal holdings from my inheritance. Notwithstanding my success as an attorney, a legislator, and a social leader, I still look upon tobacco and wheat farming as my chief area of interest. In agriculture, I see the salvation and independence of man, for "agriculture is the most useful of the occupations of man."[50] I believe that "the greatest service which can be rendered to any country is to*

add a useful plant to its culture, especially a bread-grain; next in value to bread, is oil.[51]

Thomas Jefferson refers to oil as being a useful plant byproduct, as with vegetable or olive oil for cooking and dressing food. Animal fat was commonly used in cooking in those days, but Jefferson believed it be rather unhealthy in comparison.

Thomas Jefferson often paid his clients' upfront fees to the Clerk's Office out of his own pocket. The fees were necessary in order for a case to proceed, and many times, the client did not have the money to pay the clerk at the onset of the case. Thomas Jefferson, like many lawyers of the day, may have paid the fees on behalf of his client, and be out-of-pocket for some months before the client was able to pay him from the settlement, if the case was won.

As it pertained to his law practice and the supervising of the Shadwell plantation, Thomas Jefferson was most methodical. During this time, he kept extremely detailed ledgers of all personal expenses and those of the plantation.

By 1766, he had already begun the first of several books where he recorded events, thoughts, and interests. One such book, the Garden Book, noted dates of planting fruits, vegetables, trees, and ornamentals… when they sprouted, bloomed, and when they were ready for harvest. This book would be widely used by Thomas Jefferson when designing his gardens and orchards at Monticello. He once wrote, "There is not a sprig of grass that shoots uninteresting to me."[52] As a careful observer of his environment, he also kept a lifelong record of such things as temperature, weather, expenses, recipes, and anything else that struck him as noteworthy.

Thomas Jefferson envisioned a nation of independent farmers. As a boy, his father taught him that the tobacco crop was the principal crop of commercial agriculture, and he understood the process in which it was exported to its largest markets overseas. He also understood that the soil would become deplete of its nutrients if a field continued to produce only one type of crop.

Back in the 1750s, the soil at Shadwell had begun to show the worn effects of growing only one crop year after year. In order to sustain a healthy crop, Peter Jefferson diversified his plantation by introducing crop rotation. Besides tobacco, he grew corn and wheat, which allowed nature to replenish the depleted nutrients in the soil. Farming was becoming more advanced through the growing knowledge of science and technology. Thomas Jefferson knew that in order for his future business interests to grow, he would need to eventually improve efficiency and productivity on the plantation.

Peter Jefferson most likely gave his older son instruction in surveying, and Thomas Jefferson did not let the surveying skills that he learned decay. He most certainly used them to map his land and measure his landscape at Monticello. Thomas Jefferson's architectural education had largely been developed by reading books, namely the *Four Books of Architecture* by sixteen-century architect Andrea Palladio. By May 15, 1768, at the age of twenty-five, he had contracted to level a 250-foot square area of the already gentle top of the 987-foot-high mountain, for the main dwelling at Monticello. By the end of 1768, the Monticello mountaintop was cleared, leveled, and ready for construction.

Beginning in 1769, the first bricks were being made on the premises, and the vegetable gardens were being designed. Within the year, local white masons and their apprentices, carpenters, as well as several Monticello slaves, had begun construction of the structure Thomas Jefferson used as his office, later known as the Honeymoon Cottage or the South Pavilion at Monticello.

In a letter written to his friend James Ogilvie in 1771, Thomas Jefferson wrote,

> "I have lately removed to the mountain...I have here but one room which, like the coblers', serves me for parlour, for kitchen and hall. I may add, for bed chamber and study too. My friends sometimes take a temperate dinner with me and then retire to look for beds elsewhere. I have hope, however, of getting more elbow room this summer."

Thomas Jefferson had big dreams of living a comfortable and convenient lifestyle, but he also possessed the drive and determination to realize them. He knew that his dreams could not be realized without the help of the slave population. Although Thomas hated slavery and believed that everyone had the right to be free, he was conditioned to the necessity, convenience, and importance of having them.

Chapter XXIII:
Shadwell Fire

On February 22, 1770, the Purdie and Dixon *Virginia Gazette* reported,

> "We hear from Albemarle County that about a fortnight ago the houfe of Thomas Jefferson, Eq; in that county, was burnt to the ground, together with all his furniture, books, papers &c. by which that Gentleman fultains a very great lofs. He was from home when the accident happened."

Masthead of Virginia Gazette, Purdie & Dixon edition, February 22, 1770, and the Detail of excerpt about burning of Jefferson's house, Virginia Gazette, Purkie & Dixon edition, February 22, 1770, page 3
The Colonial Williamsburg Foundation

How well I remember the catastrophe that struck my family's home at Shadwell. At the time, Mother was 50 years old, Elizabeth was 25, and still living at home due to her deficiency and inability to care for herself. Lucy was 17, and the twins were 14.

Four and ½ years ago, on the afternoon of February 1, 1770, after having dinner with my family, I departed Shadwell for "a visit to a neighbor."[53] *While there, a frenzied slave rode up to tell me that Shadwell was burning. Off in the distance, a billow of smoke was visible rising above the tree tops. I left immediately. Riding up the hill to the house, I saw Old Tobey, Jupiter and the men anxiously working to fight the fire, but to no avail. It was too far gone to save. I anxiously asked if any of my books had been saved, but the reply was, "No master, all burnt, but we save your fiddle."*

All our household items and furniture, except for several beds, perished in the blaze, including the cherry desk and bookcase in father's office, and the walnut desk and bookcase in the hall that he bequeathed to me. Mother's square tea table, the black leather storage trunk, as well as artifacts that Chief Ostenaco brought father for allowing his tribe to camp on our land, also perished. All the irreplaceable journals, field notes, maps and account books bequeathed to me by father were destroyed.

Now gone were all my early writings and papers, some cherished notebooks, my college texts, and all "my books on common law, of which I have but one left, at that time lent out. All of these, whether public or private, of business or amusement have perished in the flames."[54] *The fire also destroyed all the irreplaceable family records and account books, the journal that father kept while on expeditions, his reference books, maps, field notes, and his treasured books of literature and poetry. I deeply mourned the crushing loss of "every paper I had in the world, and almost every book. On a reasonable estimate I calculate the cost of the books burned to have been £200 sterling."[55]*

The late Peter Jefferson's entire 49-volume library perished in the fire. Also destroyed were his collection on history, religion, astronomy, law, horticulture, gardening, planting, natural philosophy, practical skills, and those relating to his duties as magistrate. Jane Jefferson's Bible, which documented the record of family births and deaths, also perished.

The few books that did survive were my Garden Book, Commonplace Book, and a few books on English Common Law. The ordeal was devastating, and I was most distressed about losing my library. My intention had always been to have a library at Monticello as prestigious and extensive as that of George Wythe's or even that of Peyton Randolph's.

No one suggested that the fire was set deliberately. I was told that the flames got out of control quickly, and were then too difficult to put out. The great destruction of the house could have been blamed on the alarm and confusion of the slaves once the fire began. I questioned the overseers and slaves, and never wanted to assume that the fire was due to malice of a disgruntled slave, but, unfortunately, that is always in the back of one's mind.

Every slave owner knew the possible dangers of a fire set deliberately. Even those slaveholders that tried to avoid violence, at some point, relied on the whip. The weak had their weapons, from sabotage to purposely spoiling the food, to even poison. Many planters feared the possibilities of conspiracies, or worse, revolts, on a plantation, but in the case of Shadwell, there was no reported indication of this.

> *It was said that if father was still alive, the fire would not have happened, since he was meticulously attentive to the fires of our everyday life. Mother and the kitchen staff were always on the alert to avoid a cooking or heating fire that could burst in a flash, and it was always a possibility that a neglected chimney or hearth could create a flaming rebellion. I often feel guilty for not being present to prevent the fire and protect my family and home, but I am very thankful to God that my family was able to escape without injury.*
>
> *I thought it best to send Randolph, who was 14 at the time, off to the home and care of family nearby until he was of age to leave for William & Mary in the fall of the following year. I quickly arranged for a smaller house to be built at Shadwell, while mother, Elizabeth, and Anna took up residence in the overseer's house. I boarded at the tavern in Charlottesville until the south pavilion at Monticello was suitable for me to move into.*

Mary Jefferson married John Bolling on January 24, 1760, and they lived at Fairfields in Goochland County and Lickinghole Creek, just west of the Goochland

Courthouse. Martha Jefferson married Dabney Carr on July 20, 1765, and lived at Spring Forest in Goochland County. Lucy Jefferson had married her first cousin, Charles Lilburne Lewis, on September 12, 1769, and they lived on a tract of land south of the Rivanna, not far from Shadwell. The Jefferson daughters and their husbands, no doubt, offered assistance at Shadwell in their family's time of need.

Randolph was sent to live with his mother's sister Mary Randolph Lewis and her husband Charles Lewis, Jr., and was schooled by Benjamin Snead at the Lewis plantation at Buck Island. When he turned sixteen, Randolph attended The Grammar School at The College of William & Mary, continued on as a student at the college, and resided there from October 1771 until September 1773.

On November 26, 1770, I moved into the south pavilion, which was the only finished structure at Monticello. This allowed me to continue to oversee construction of the main house, design of the terraced vegetable garden, as well as keep a watchful eye over Shadwell's plantation production, which still is the lifeline of our family, and instrumental in funding the construction costs at Monticello.

Chapter XXIV: Martha Wayles Skelton

In December 1770, over two years after the death of her husband, I began courting my Patty, a nickname given to her by her father. I originally met Martha in Williamsburg when she was married to lawyer and planter Bathurst Skelton, who, years earlier, had been a classmate of mine at William & Mary. After they married in 1766, they lived at Elk Hill, Bathurst's plantation on Byrd Creek in Goochland County, on the north side of the James River, opposite Elk Island. Less than a year later, Martha and Bathurst had their only son and named him John. After Bathurst's unexpected death in 1768, Martha and young John, then three years old, moved back to her father's plantation in Charles City County, The Forest, where Martha was born and raised.

Patty is a woman of extraordinary beauty, both in form and face. A little above middle height, she is delicate, well poised, gentle, with a queen-like carriage, and is graced with a warm-affectionate disposition. Her abundant hair is the most admired shade of auburn. Her complexion is fair, and her hazel eyes are large and expressive. Patty is charming, well educated, has a delicate singing voice, and plays the pianoforte with uncommon skill. She possesses habits of good society, and has the uncanny ability to welcome my family and friends to perfection. Patty is a gracious hostess, honorable in all her ways, and an industrious housewife, knowing much about raising and educating children, as well as caring for the sick. Besides being the supervisor over the household servants and all their responsibilities, she has a knack for preserving food, recipes, and cooking. She sews, spins, weaves, knits, enjoys making soap and candles, and also accompanies me while working in the garden.

After the fire at Shadwell, I fervently began to rebuild my personal library, for I just "cannot live without books."[56] Within three years of the fire, I accumulated a new collection at Monticello, totaling 1,256 volumes, which I admit proudly, has far exceeded any library of my mentors. I have acquired books from Nathaniel Walthoe, William Byrd II, and from the estates of Philip Ludwell, John Wayles, Bathurst Skelton, and my beloved mentor, George Wythe, in fine arts, religion, law, history, poetry, Christianity, and philosophy.

As evidence of George Wythe's great affection toward his protégé and unbeknownst to Thomas, George Wythe bequeathed to him on June 8, 1806, his superb library, while dying of arsenic poisoning. Thomas Jefferson would later learn of the bequest with gratitude, as well as with much anguish, once informed of the death of his eighty-year-old friend and mentor.

Throughout his life, Thomas Jefferson continued to collect books across a vast spectrum of topics and languages, which eventually totaled 6,487 books, the largest private book collection in North America. He divided his home library into such categories as Memory, Reason, and Imagination, which exemplified and spanned his multifaceted interests.

Dr. Small and George Wythe ignited a passion and affection for books in Thomas. Thomas Jefferson delighted in mastering everything, and while promoted by his self-discipline, came close to being obsessive. In turn, he tried to kindle that same fire in his friends and family by later developing a list of suggested books he thought important.

Thomas Jefferson's suggested book list, taken from a letter written from Monticello to Robert Skipwith (Patty's brother-in-law) on August 3, 1771, reads as follows:

> "Percy's *Reliques of Ancient English Poetry*," Chaucer, Shakespeare, Milton, Dryden, Spenser, Thompson, Gray, Gay, and Pope, plays by Steele, Congreve, and Addison, novels by Smollett, Richardson, Langhorne, and Sterne. He included the works of Swift, the nine-volume Spectator, the five-volume Tatler, Locke's "conduct of the mind in search of truth," Bolingbroke's five-volume "political works," Burke in eight volumes, and Hume's History of England. Moliere was on the list, Voltaire and Montesquieu, along with Buffon's natural history. From the classics, he recommended Xenophon, Epictetus, Seneca, Cicero, Livy, Sallust, Tacitus, Caesar, and Plutach. The Bible was included, though he was critical of it,

and Josephus. There were books on gardening, husbandry, painting, history, and law, Franklin's Electricity, and "A compendium of Physic & Surgery" by Nourse.[57]

Patty and I delight in stimulating conversation, and enjoy discussing popular classics in front of a crackling fire. We pursue the pleasures of reading Ovid's epic mythological poem, Metamorphoses, as well as Lawrence Stern's humorous novel, Tristram Shandy.

In the morning, I read law; and in the evening, work by historians, essayists, and poets. I enjoy books by Joseph Addison, Jonathan Swift, Alexander Pope, and especially William Shakespeare. Patty enjoys English literature and shares my love for poetry. Her favorite book is Adventures of Telemachus by Francois Fenelon, which she brought with her from The Forest.

Martha's father, John Wayles, was born in Lancaster, England, on January 31, 1715. He left his family in 1734 at the age of nineteen, and sailed alone to Virginia. By the age of thirty, he was an established lawyer, slave trader, business agent for a tobacco exporting firm, and a wealthy plantation owner. John Wayles married twenty-five-year-old Martha Eppes on May 3, 1746, a widow from the town of Bermuda Hundred (the eastern portion of Chesterfield County). They resided at The Forest, his 411-acre thriving tobacco and wheat plantation located in the Tidewater region along the James River, not far from Williamsburg.

Seven and a half months later, on December 23, 1746, Martha Eppes gave birth to twins. The girl was stillborn and the boy lived only a few hours. Almost two years later, on October 30, 1748. Martha Eppes gave birth to her only surviving child, a daughter they named Martha. Less than a week later, on November 5, 1748, Martha Eppes Wayles died at the age of twenty-seven, due to complications from that birth. Betty Hemings, a thirteen-year-old enslaved girl, was put in charge of helping care for the infant at the time of Martha Eppes's untimely death. John Wayles would remarry twice more, and bury two more wives during young Martha's upbringing.

John Wayles and his second wife, Tabitha (Mary) Cocke, had four daughters, the first dying at infancy. Young Martha's surviving stepsisters were Elizabeth, Tabitha, and Anne. Tabitha Cocke died sometime between August 1756 and January 1760. John Wayles married his third wife, Elizabeth Lomax Skelton in January 1760, having no children with her. Elizabeth Lomax Skelton Wayles died a little over a year after their marriage, on February 10, 1761.

Young Martha received a basic education at home, which focused on the domestic arts, but received further education through private tutors in the areas of literature, music, dancing, Bible, and French. She enjoyed poetry and fiction, was very literate and well read.

Through her father's third wife, Martha met Bathurst Skelton, the brother of Elizabeth Skelton's deceased first husband, Reuben Skelton, and they began to court. Martha married Bathurst at The Forest on November 20, 1766, a month after celebrating her eighteenth birthday. She gave birth to their first son, John, on November 7, 1767. Tragically, on September 30, 1768, Bathurst died of an unexpected illness, leaving Martha a widow at the age of nineteen, only one year and ten months after they married. Martha and her young son moved back to The Forest to remain in the care of her wealthy father.

Chapter XXV:
Courting "Patty"

It is not certain how Thomas Jefferson originally met Martha. It is possible that they may have met at a social engagement that Bathurst and she attended in Williamsburg, or possibly at the home of their maestro, while he and Martha were coming and going from their music lessons. What is certain is that after the mourning of her late husband, and the appropriate time had passed, Martha attracted many suitors from the Tidewater society. She was not without a lack of gentlemen callers, young and old, who sought her hand in marriage. Thomas Jefferson was one of them, a successful planter and lawyer with his own large practice and a member of the House of Burgesses representing Albemarle County.

When Thomas first came to woo the lovely widow, he was twenty-eight years old, square shouldered, six feet two inches tall, and straight bodied. He was a lean man with a ruddy complexion, reddish hair, hazel eyes, long face, and a high nose. He carried himself with grace and vigor, and he appeared intelligent with a friendly nature. Thomas's wealth, high rank in his profession, his excellent character, and his agreeable appearance, made him an appropriate suitor. Among all Martha's suitors, Thomas was her favorite. Thomas Jefferson found Martha especially attractive because of her education and her penchant for music.

> *As our courtship progressed, on the 20th of February, 1771, I commissioned the purchase of a German clavichord for Martha. Before it was scheduled to be shipped, I wrote Thomas Adams in London requesting him to order me a pianoforte instead, specifying that "I wanted it made from solid mahogany, not veneer, and stipulated that its workmanship be very handsome and worthy the acceptance of a lady for whom I intended it."*[58]

Mohogany Square English Pianoforte by
Johannes Zumpe, London, 1766
The Colonial Williamsburg Foundation

> *At first, I was worried that my strong feelings toward Martha were not mutual, and expressed my concerns to our mutual friend, Mrs. Drummond. I received a letter of encouragement from Mrs.*

Drummond dated March 12, 1771, advising me to persevere, also stating that Martha had "good sense, and good nature," After reading the letter, I felt my fear was not warranted. Mrs. Drummond also hoped that Martha would not refuse my love, and closed her letter by stating that she suspected that Martha's heart was already "engaged."

Here is an excerpt from Mrs. Drummond's letter:

Wmsburgh. March 12th

"…persever thou, good Young Man, persevere.—She has good Sence, and good Nature, and I hope wil not refuse (the Blessing shal' I say) why not as I think it,—of Yr. hand, if her Hearts, not ingagd allready. …I most sincearly wish You, the full completion, of all Yr. wishes, both as to the Lady and everything else—"

Once I knew that the pianoforte was delivered to The Forest, I paid Martha a visit one afternoon. Coincidentally and unknowingly, we were later told that two rivals arrived at Martha's house at the same time, and were shown into the parlor. As she played the pianoforte, I accompanied her on my violin in the drawing room, and we young lovers sang a tender melody to each other. The rivals listened for a few moments, and then left, never to return.

I remember telling a friend, "In every scheme of happiness she is placed in the fore-ground of the picture, as the principal figure. Take that away and it is no picture for me."[59] I had become so enamo-

red with Martha that I could hardly imagine life without her.

Our blissfulness would soon turn to heartache, when on the 10th of June 1771, Martha's four year old son, John, died of fever. I was in Williamsburg at the time word arrived of his death, and immediately went to comfort Martha and her family at The Forest. John's death at such a tender age, just a few years after the death of her first husband, was heartbreaking for Martha, and I allowed her the necessary time she needed to mourn. In July, I met with John Wayles to discuss my marriage intentions, and he graciously gave me his consent and blessing. At the proper time, I respectfully asked Martha for her hand in marriage, and, to my delight, she accepted.

In late December 1771, I left Monticello for The Forest to visit with Martha and her family. While there, the husband of Martha's sister Elizabeth, Francis Eppes, and I drew up the bond for the marriage license, and we both signed it on December 23rd. One week later, I purchased the marriage license in Williamsburg, and returned to The Forest to help Martha prepare for our wedding.

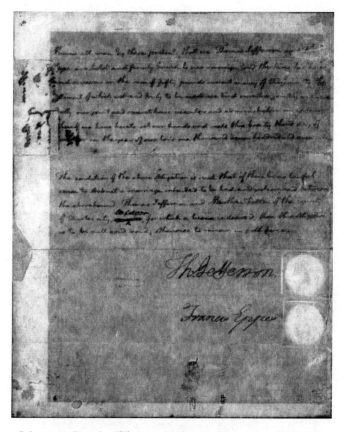

Marriage Bond of Thomas Jefferson, December 23, 1771
The Library of Virginia
Reproduction courtesy of The Colonial
Williamsburg Foundation
*Note that the word "spinster" is erased, and
"widow" is inserted in another handwriting.

The license-bond for the marriage, demanded by the laws of Virginia, written by Jefferson's own hand, reads as follows:

23 Dec 1771

Know all men by these presents that we Thomas Jefferson and Francis Eppes are held and firmly bound to our sovereign lord the king his heirs and successors in the sum of fifty pounds current money of Virginia, to the paiment of which, well and truly to be made we bind ourselves jointly and severally, our joint and several heirs executors and administrators in witness whereof we have hereto set our hands and seals this twenty third day of December in the year of our lord one thousand seven hundred and seventy one.

The condition of above obligation is such that if there be no lawful cause to obstruct a marriage intended to be had and solemnized between the abovebound Thomas Jefferson and Martha Skelton of the county of Charles City, Widow*, for which a license is desired, then this obligation is to be null and void; otherwise to remain in full force.

TH: JEFFERSON
FRANCIS EPPES[60]

In colonial times, "marriage banns" were usually the formal process leading up to a wedding. Notice of the impending marriage was read from the local church pulpit or posted on the church door over a set period of time. The purpose of this was to allow those who knew the bride and groom to object if there was a legal reason why the marriage should not take place. Three legal barriers were: either or both were not of legal age, either or both were already married, or the bride and groom were too closely related to marry under the laws of the jurisdiction.

As more colonists gradually located west into the frontier, often either the bride or groom would not be well known in the community. To overcome this, the "marriage bond" or "wedding bond" as Thomas Jefferson referred to it, soon replaced the "marriage banns." The groom, Thomas Jefferson, and a suitable bondsman, Francis Eppes, would pledge a monetary amount to an official, often the governor, as a guarantee that there were no legal impediments to the forth coming marriage. The bond amount was conditional, which meant that the pledged amount would be forfeited if there was proof of a legal reason the couple should not marry. If no legal reason existed, the bond would be null and void.

Chapter XXVI:
Married Life

"On the first of January 1772, I was married to Martha Wayles Skelton, widow of Bathurst Skelton, and daughter of John Wayles, then 23 years old." [61] *My ailing father-in-law hosted the elaborate holiday wedding at his plantation home in grand and liberal style. Fiddlers were hired from afar, and many tables were spread out for scores of family and guests inside the mansion.*

Anglican ministers, Reverend Davis and Reverend Coutts, performed the ceremony, but Reverend Davis effectually tied the knot and was the officiating clergyman. Since childhood, Martha remained very close with the Eppes family that lived nearby, and she enjoyed introducing me to all her many relatives. The festivities continued for over two weeks before we left for the 100 mile journey to our new home at Monticello. "The portion which came on that event to Mrs. Jefferson, after the debts were paid, which were very considerable, was about equal to my own patrimony, and consequently doubled the ease of our circumstances."[62]

When Thomas Jefferson married the young widow, Martha brought to their household a number of items acquired during her first marriage to Bathurst Skelton, besides some personal furniture that was eventually delivered. On January 18, 1772, Thomas Jefferson made a list in his Fee Book, "By sundry European goods on hand at the death of B. Skelton & taken by me."[63] The list mentions many household items, including one silver ladle, one dozen tablespoons, one dozen teaspoons, two pairs of "gaderoon salts"[64] with four glass liners, and four "salt shovels."[65]

After a hearty breakfast on the morning of January 18th, we bid farewell and departed in our two horse drawn covered phaeton, as a light snow began to fall. The roads leading from The Forest were passable, but the journey became increasingly difficult west of Richmond on our way to Tuckahoe, where we were expected to overnight. Upon our arrival, we were graciously welcomed to stay as long as was necessary for the travel conditions to improve. During dinner, we delighted in reminiscing about my childhood years at Tuckahoe, and afterward, spent the evening enjoying music and dance in the central salon.

As I was reacquainting myself with the house, I discovered that the narrow yellow pine steps leading downstairs to the servant's kitchen were now too small for my much larger feet. Martha and I slept upstairs in the beautifully appointed bedchamber that was once my nursery, just across the landing from what was my parent's bedchamber. I laughed when I saw the bed warmer that my mother had accidentally left at Tuckahoe nearly 20 years earlier, resting alongside the fireplace.

The next morning the wind had subsided, and Martha and I road our horses through the snow-dusted boxwood garden, and visited the family cemetery. I was surprised to notice that the schoolhouse that father built was much smaller and closer to the main house than I remembered.

After we visited at Tuckahoe for a time, Martha and I decided it was best we continue our journey, and planned for a morning departure. The household servants loaded out bags onto the phaeton, along with warmed blankets, and a small chest of food, which consisted of some cold fowl, ham, biscuits, and fruit. We thanked my family for hosting us, and extended an invitation for them to visit us in the fall. Martha and I departed down the cedar lined lane and proceeded on our way to Monticello.

From Tuckahoe, the Jefferson's would have ridden west on Three Notch'd Road until they arrived at the intersection of Three Notch'd Road and Martin King's Road (near present day Zion Crossroads in Fluvanna County). There, they turned southwest on to Martin King's Road until it intersected with Carter Mountain Road (Virginia State Route 20 today) at Carter's Bridge. After a necessary stop, they traveled on Carter Mountain Road for eight miles until they reached the entranceway to Monticello. Forging up their long, snow-laden mountain drive, they finally arrived home.

While traveling through a snow storm, just eight miles from Monticello, our phaeton bogged down, stalling in three feet of snow at Carter's Bridge. I unhitched our two horses, left the phaeton at

Carter's Bridge, and we forged a short distance to seek assistance at Edward Carter's nearby plantation claim house, Blenheim, on the Hardware River. The farm overseer graciously welcomed us in to warm ourselves. As a courtesy, the good man offered to retrieve our phaeton, and have it repaired by Colonel Carter's carriage maker, Davy Watson, then insisted on lending us two of his own horses for the remaining eight mile journey. After a pleasant, but brief respite, we continued on to Monticello through the cold and moonlit night. I eventually sent a servant down to Blenheim to retrieve the phaeton, and exchanged the Carter horses for our own.

Blenheim Claim House
Courtesy of Blenheim Vineyards, Charlottesville, Virginia

In 1730, Edward Carter's father, John Carter of Shirley Plantation in Charles City County (son of land baron Robert "King" Carter of Corotoman Plantation in Lancaster County) obtained a patent for 9,350 acres of Goochland County land as a crown grant from King George II, as the Secretary of the Virginia Colony. The large tract embraced the whole of what is still called Carter Mountain, as well as the Blenheim property, in what later became the southern part of Albemarle County in 1744. In order to establish ownership of the 9,350 acres, John Carter was obliged, by law, to clear a section of land and build a "claim house" within the first three years, or lose claim to the land. In order to fulfill the contract with the British crown, John Carter had a four-room, two-story cottage constructed, called it Blenheim Farm, and put a farm overseer in charge.

The Blenheim plantation produced mostly tobacco and cotton, and was named after one of the finest and most elegant homes in England, Blenheim Palace in Woodstock, which still stands today outside of Oxford. Upon the death of John Carter in 1742, the entire 9,350-acre tract was bequeathed to his son Edward Carter, who eventually took up residence there. Edward Carter was not on the property on the evening that Thomas and Martha sought assistance at Blenheim. It was Edward Carter's overseer who graciously invited them in to warm themselves, and lent them fresh horses for the remainder of the trip.

Today, the original Blenheim Claim House is situated on the property of Blenheim Vineyards (See Appendix V.) in Albemarle County's attractive estate and vineyard community. It is still considered Albemarle County's oldest home. (www.blenheimvineyards.com)

Snow continued to fall as we rode up the mountain slope, and it quickly increased in depth. It was the deepest snowfall we had ever experienced in Albemarle County. The eight mile trek from Blenheim was windy and cold, slow-going, treacherous in spots, but, nonetheless, beautiful.

Late that night, exhausted from our dreary journey and penetrated by the cold, we reached Monticello, only to find that the house was dark, and no fire burning. The servants had not suspected our late arrival, and all had retired to their own cabins for the night. What a sorry welcome for Mrs. Jefferson, but by the grace of God, we arrived home safely through one of the worst snowstorms to ever hit Virginia.

I escorted my bride inside her new abode, lit a fire in the fireplace, and proceeded to lead the horses to the stable for the night. Returning back to the warmth of the cottage, I groped about for something to eat or drink. I remembered the half bottle of wine that I had hidden behind some books on my bookshelf, and it became our only supper. We toasted our new home, nicknaming it our honeymoon cottage, and merrily enjoyed the rest of the evening with song and laughter. Unfortunately, we were unable to retrieve Patty's personal belongings and all her books until the snow had somewhat melted. Our first daughter, Martha, nicknamed "Patsy," was born nine months later.

The house to which Thomas Jefferson brought his bride was not a spacious and elegant mansion. It was no larger, or any more attractive, than the average attendant's lodge. The couple settled into the one room, eighteen-by-eighteen square brick building, which originally served as Thomas Jefferson's office. The cottage would be their home until Jefferson's workers were able to complete the north wing of the main house later that year. Thomas and Martha decided to be as happy in it as any couple could be. As a husband, Thomas was devoted to Martha, so much so that he tended, at times, to neglect his professional career in favor of domestic pleasures. Martha was devoted to her husband and their marriage was peculiarly happy.

Chapter XXVII:
A Tribute to Dabney

Thomas Jefferson takes a break from his writing to stand up and walk about in order to improve the circulation in his legs. He checks on Cucullin and gives him a handful of oats, then removes the canteen from his saddlebag. After taking a swig of water, he places the canteen back, then gropes inside the saddlebag for the spare inkpot. Thomas Jefferson returns to his rock, and continues to write.

> *Before I left Monticello earlier this morning, I advised Patty not to expect me at any certain time, since I never know how long I will be detained at Shadwell. I usually spend time with mother, check the gristmill and brewery operations, speak to the overseers about the overall condition of the plantation, and inspect the outbuildings for needed repairs before leaving. Since today is the anniversary of father's death, I feel the need for personal time to reflect on my family and friends, meditate on my good fortune, and enjoy this peaceful solitude.*
>
> *Recently, I have been thinking a great deal about Dabney, our friendship, and all the times we had spent roaming the forest trails of Shadwell and Monticello. As a young man, he had always been*

very fond of my sister, Martha, and after realizing that the feelings were mutual, they began to court. After an appropriate amount of time and his respectful request for her hand in marriage, I gave them my blessing and consent.

At age 22, Dabney was already a delegate in the House of Burgesses, and Martha was 19 when they both married at Shadwell on July 20, 1765. After the wedding, the newlyweds moved to Dabney's home, Spring Forest, in Goochland County, "…a very small house, with a table, half a dozen chairs, and one or two servants"[66] to begin their life together and start a family. Their first child, Jean, was born in 1766, twins Lucy and Mary in 1768, Peter in 1770, and Samuel in 1771.

I was in Williamsburg when the birth of their sixth child drew near. Dabney was expected to join me in Williamsburg to attend a special session of the House of Burgesses in mid-April, for what would be his first and last speech. Since Martha was nearing the end of her pregnancy, Dabney thought it was best to bring her and their five children to Shadwell to be in mother's care during his absence.

In early May of last year, just a few days after Dabney returned from Williamsburg, Martha gave birth to their sixth child, naming him after Dabney. A few weeks later, he set out once again for Williamsburg. As was reported, Dabney was not far from Shadwell when he was suddenly stricken with dysentery, a high fever accompanied by nausea. He was taken back to Shadwell, and mother called our family physician, Dr. George Gilmer, who diagnosed Dabney with bilious fever. The course of the disease was violent and brief, insomuch that he could not be moved to his home at Spring Forest. On May 16, 1773, at about 12 o'clock in the afternoon, my dear friend Dabney died at the age of 30, leaving my sister a widow with five children and an infant, Dabney's namesake.

I took Dabney's sudden death very poorly, especially since I was still in Williamsburg when his death occurred. Mother was worried that the fever would spread throughout the family, so she arranged for Dabney's quick burial on the Shadwell grounds. When I returned on the 21st of May, I had his body disinterred and moved to a gravesite beneath our favorite oak tree at Monticello. I then sent for Reverend Charles Clay of St. Anne's Parish to perform the funeral service.

I honored my dearest friend by composing an epitaph, and arranging a formal burial to be performed where we spent many hours of our youth. Dabney and I had a boyhood pact that the first one to die would be buried by the survivor under our favorite oak tree, and it was my supreme honor to fulfill his wishes. I sent for a copper plate to be nailed on the tree at the foot of his grave with this inscription:

> *"Still shall thy grave with ris-*
> *ing flowers be dressed*
> *And the green turf be lightly on thy breast;*
> *There shall the morn her earliest tears bestow,*
> *There the 1st roses of the year shall blow,*
> *While angels with their silver wings o'ershade*
> *The ground now sacred by*
> *thy reliques made."[67]*

After the funeral service, I spent the next few days with my bereaved sister at Spring Forest. Dabney's death fell with stunning force on Martha, who, I was told, had also been ill when Dabney set out on his last journey to Williamsburg. Apparently, after she bid him her final farewell, Martha raised herself up from her sick couch to catch a parting glance of Dabney as he rode past the window; but she merely saw his hat moving. For weeks and months, whether in the blaze of noon day or in the darkness of night, Martha said that the moving-phantom hat was ever passing before her eyes. Knowing how inseparable Dabney and I were, Martha graciously gave me some of his favorite books for my library.

Dabney Carr was the first to be buried at the Monticello burial ground. Thomas's emotionally wrought inscription for Dabney's grave marker reads as follows:

HERE LIE THE REMAINS OF
DABNEY CARR,
SON OF
JOHN AND BARBARA CARR,
OF LOUISA COUNTY VA.
BORN OCTOBER 26, 1743.
INTERMARRIED JULY 20, 1765,
WITH
MARTHA JEFFERSON,
DAUGHTER OF

**PETER AND JANE RANDOLPH
JEFFERSON.
DIED MAY 16, 1773
AT CHARLOTTESVILLE VA.**

**LAMENTED SHADE!
WHOM EVERY GIFT OF HEAVEN
PROFUSELY BLEST,
A TEMPER WINNING MILD,
NOR PITY SOFTER,
NOR WAS TRUTH MORE BRIGHT;
CONSTANT IN DOING
WELL, HE NEITHER SOUGHT
NOR SHUNNED APPLAUSE.**

**NO BASHFUL MERIT SIGHED
NEAR HIM NEGLECTED
SYMPATHISING HE WIPED OFF
THE TEAR FROM SORROW'S
CLOUDED EYE AND WITH
KINDLY HAND TAUGHT
HER HEART TO SMILE.**

**TO HIS VIRTUE, GOOD SENSE,
LEARNING AND FRIENDSHIP,
THIS STONE IS DEDICATED BY
THOMAS JEFFERSON
WHO OF ALL MEN LOVED HIM MOST** [68]

Dr. George Gilmer settled in Charlottesville in 1771 for the purpose of practicing medicine. He married Lucy Walker, the daughter of Dr. Thomas Walker of Castle Hill, and became a prominent physician in the area, counting both the Jefferson and Madison families amongst his patients. Following the custom of that time, Dr. Gilmer was also active in politics, having served with distinction in the House of Burgesses in the stormy years preceding the Revolution.

Chapter XXVIII:
Remembering Dabney

Dabney's character was of a high order. A spotless integrity, sound judgment, handsome imagination, enriched by education and reading, quick and clear in his conceptions, of correct and ready elocution, impressing every hearer with the sincerity of the heart from which it flowed... The number of his friends, and the warmth of their affection, were proofs of his worth, and of their estimate of it.[69]

My dear friend's death was unexpected and untimely, and the goals we shared under our favorite oak tree near the summit of Monticello, some of which will never be realized. When we were boys, we were the best of comrades. On many a weekend break from the Maury School, and throughout most of the summer, Dabney visited me at Shadwell. We would take our books, some food, set out early in the morning and ride our horses along the edge of the tobacco field, then down to the Rivanna.

After crossing at the ford, we would hike up the beautiful forest trail dotted with dogwood and red bud trees, until we arrived at our usual spot, the rustic seat we had constructed deep in the woods, far away from the sight and hearing of man. Together, we studied Henry de Bracton, Sir Edward Coke, and Matthew Bacon, while we discussed the present political situation, and painted the glowing visions of our future.

Henry de Bracton was a thirteenth-century leading Medieval English judge and author, famous for his writings on English Law, and his ideas on "mens rea" (criminal intent). Sir Edward Coke was a British judge and politician who defended British common law and its constitution. Matthew Bacon was an eighteenth century author and commentator of the laws of England. His work, *A New Abridgment of the Law*, a standard law text, was a collection of court cases that were of interest to lawyers looking for precedents, and described them in abridged form.

I remember the day I shared with Dabney my desire to someday build a home on that very spot. When I reminisce about Dabney, I think of how "friendship is precious, not only in the shade, but in the sunshine of life, and thanks to a benevolent arrangement, the greater part of life is sunshine.[70]

It saddens me that Dabney's children will grow up without a father, and that his youngest son and namesake will never know the wonderful man that I called my friend. Jean is now 8, Lucy and Mary are both 6, Peter is 4, Samuel is 3, and little Dabney is just over a year. In an effort to support Martha and her six children, I have extended an invitation for them to stay at Monticello, which she does from time to time. When Martha visits, she is a great help to Patty, since the recoveries from

Patty's two pregnancies were somewhat slow and difficult. Martha helps us with our girls, and we all enjoy watching the cousins play together. It is my desire that she and the children eventually move to Monticello, and I have expressed this sentiment to her.

Chapter XXIX:
Death and Debt

Twelve days after Dabney's death, tragedy struck again. On May 28, 1773, John Wayles, Patty's long-time ailing father, died of bilious fever at the age of 58. We brought him to Monticello and laid him to rest in the graveyard. As a result, Patty and I gained access to a very large inheritance, and a considerable amount of property. Patty was left approximately 11,800 acres of land, which roughly included The Forest, the 411 acre working planta-tion where she was born and raised, its 135 slaves, as well as other large tracts along the James River: the 2,042 acres at Judith Creek, the 4,800 acre Poplar Forest plantation in Bedford County, and the 1,076-acre Willis Creek plantation and its slaves.

In addition to Patty's share in the division of the estate, she came into possession of two properties which her father had held as "curtesy tenure" (land he obtained as a result of a previous wife's death); 330 acres at Elk Island to which she had dower rights from her first husband, Bathurst Skelton, and the 1,200 acres at Indian Camp that she inherited through her mother, Martha Eppes.

In the eighteen months between our marriage and Mr. Wayles' death, I watched the family fortune turn sour amidst a series of his bad business deals, not all of which were sound. Besides inheriting his holdings, we also inherited the majority of his debt. In order to pay the creditors, I immediately began the process of selling over half of the land, and slaves as necessary, which included the Judith Creek, Indian Camp, and Willis Creek plantations.

Thankfully, all the properties, except for the land swap of Elk Hill plantation in Goochland County, Elk Island, and the Poplar Forest plantation in Bedford County, were liquidated as of January 26th of this year. Martha and I wanted to keep the small brick home at Elk Hill as a 2nd residence since it is only about 35 miles east of Monticello, as well as Elk Island, which is surrounded with plentiful game and excellent for hunting parties.

Poplar Forest is a well-watered and productive 4,800 acre working farm which John Wayles settled in the 1760s using a small number of slaves. Under the direction of an overseer, the slaves cut down trees to create fields and began planting hills of tobacco around the stumps. The plantation is doing very well, and I can manage it from Monticello. It will provide me with a significant income, and pose for a delightful family retreat, at some point. I have paid off the creditors, and have been funneling the extra finances into the continued construction costs at Monticello.

"Mr. Wayles was a lawyer of much practice, to which he was introduced more by his great industry, punctuality, and practical readiness, than to eminence in the science of his profession. He was a most agreeable companion, full of pleasantry and good humor, and welcomed in every society..."[71]

Beyond the philosophical complications that slavery possessed at the time, Thomas Jefferson's troubles as a slave owner became more complicated as a result of a poor personal choice that his deceased father-in-law made. Like many widowed aristocrats in Virginia, John Wayles had turned to one of his female slaves, Betty Hemings, for comfort and companionship toward the end of his life. Betty Hemings gradually found herself locked in as the long-term mistress to her master, John Wayles. She bore six of her twelve children by him: Robert, James, Thenia, Critta, Peter, and Sarah (nicknamed Sally). Thomas Jefferson not only inherited the financial holdings of John Wayles, but he found himself in the complicated situation of possessing half-siblings of his spouse, Martha.

Chapter XXX:
Earthquakes of 1774

This past winter, Albemarle County experienced unusually bitter wind, heavy thunder storms, and earthquakes. It was Monday, the 21st of February, at 2:11pm, when "the first recorded earthquake in Virginia was felt… and it caused considerable alarm, but almost no damage."[72] I happened to be working in Charlottesville at the time, and immediately left to check on my family at Monticello and Shadwell.

While riding home, "another shock of the earthquake occurred at 2:45 pm…, just as violent, but not as long."[73] Mother said that the land beneath the wood-frame structures at Shadwell "shook the homes so sensibly that everyone ran out of doors."[74] The natural phenomena confused and concerned my family, especially Elizabeth, who kept asking mother to allow her to stay with us at Monticello. Mother reassured Elizabeth that her new home was sturdy and safe, and that no harm would come to her.

The following afternoon, Shadwell "felt the shock of the earthquake again at 2pm"[75] which shook dishes off mother's cabinet shelves, breaking onto the floor. It was said that Elizabeth became so frightened, that she ran out of the house and down to the river in an attempt to cross, in an effort to flee to the safety of Monticello. She was followed by Jupiter's 22 year old sister, Little Sall, who did not want to leave Bet unattended. While they both attempted to cross the Rivanna in our skiff, the swift moving water overturned it. The flooding and elevated water level of the Rivanna was most likely due to the heavy rain the previous days. That flood was "the highest ever known, except the great fresh in May 1771, when our gristmill at Shadwell was swept away."[76]

Feeling the earthquake in Charlottesville, I, again, hastily returned to the house. Jupiter and the other men were out frantically searching for Bet and Little Sall when I arrived. By nightfall, we head back home, only to resume our search the next day, fighting against the chilling winds of winter. Tragically, Bet, still a child at age 29, drowned and was found two days later along the river bank on February 24th, but unfortunately, Little Sall was never found. Jupiter and his family did their best to console the grief-stricken Old Sall, while Martha stayed with mother. Aftershocks continued to vibrate the ground, as I helped my bereaved mother make the necessary arrangements with Reverend Clay for the funeral service.

It was a terrible loss for our family, and especially for Old Sall, Jupiter, and Little Sall's children, 2 year old Cyrus and 6 year old Rachel. A somber funeral service was held for Bet on the 7th of March, and many of our local friends attended. We buried her alongside father's grave at Shadwell, and later had a memorial service for Little Sall. To this day, I regret not being at Shadwell to reassure and protect my family.

Again, out of respect for my family, Reverend Clay did not want to accept the 40 shillings for his services, but, I persuaded him to accept a different offer. Instead, I "sold my two old book cases to Mr. Clay...for performing the funeral service on burying my sister Elizabeth, and more for preaching Mr. Carr's funeral sermon..."[77] last May.

Although life's tragedies seem to affect me deeply, I learned at an early age, the necessity of becoming numb to their unrelenting attacks, and for my own good, decided to follow my own philosophy to "take things always by their smooth handle." [78] I seek repose from the insurmountable stress and bouts of sadness from family loss by playing the violin, writing in my notebook, or by riding Cucullin through the country side. In times of tragedy, although difficult, I continue to rely on my strong faith and belief in God's provisions.

Chapter XXXI:
The Great Fresh of 1771

I will never forget the devastating spring we experienced in 1771. The previous winter was particularly cold. Creeks and tributaries froze, and the below freezing temperatures lasted well into early spring, until the first 10-12 days of May when we experienced torrential rains, which deluged the central Blue Ridge Mountain region. The destructive flooding from the great fresh and the continuous rain inundated the lowlands of all Virginia Rivers east of the Alleghenies. The land runoff had nowhere to go but over the banks, as the rivers could not handle the runoff fast enough.

The spring fresh of 1771 produced the worst flood waters in Virginia history, and in some areas around Scott's Landing, 40-45 feet above the mean level of the James River. For 60 hours, the James River rose continuously, as much as 16 inches per hour. Property losses were disastrous in the Piedmont, as well as in the Tidewater area. It was estimated that 4-6,000 hogshead of stored tobacco had been destroyed, and more than half of that year's spring crop of seedlings had suffered the same fate in the fields along the James and low lying plantations along the shore.

Father's gristmill at Shadwell was swept away in what was said to be, "the greatest flood ever known in Virginia." Rich top soil along the James River was washed away and buried under 10-12 feet of sand overlaid with rocks, hundreds of livestock were killed, buildings along the rivers were destroyed, crops were lost, and people drowned.

Almost all the dugout canoes used for commerce and transportation along the river for the past 30 years were destroyed in the deluge, as well as all the tobacco warehouse sheds. As a result of the flash flood, there were very few large trees left for rebuilding the dugout canoes, which severely endangered the future of Virginia's tobacco trade.

Out of necessity in rescuing the tobacco transportation industry, two brothers, Anthony and Benjamin Rucker developed a new kind of vessel, one that could be built using planks on a wood plank frame. They called these new vessels "bateaux," a term that originates from the French word *boats*.

There were several distinguishing characteristics of a batteau:

First, the batteau could be built by a carpenter, and didn't require skilled craftsmanship, making them cheap and quick to build. The materials were locally found wood, such as white pine, cedar, or oak. The fastenings were typically soft iron nails, something that could be made by any local blacksmith. The boats were sealed with pine tar, and could be rigged with a minimum of rope.

The batteaux were long, narrow, open boats, and pointed at each end. Very long planks, fastened to ribs, formed the sides and bottom. They had no keel to interfere with navigating the river rapids, which made the batteaux well adapted to shallow water. The batteaux had no rudder and were guided by long oarlike sweeps that engaged notches formed in the tip of the nose cones. They were six to eight feet wide, up to sixty feet long, and eighteen to twenty-four inches deep. The flat boats enabled weight to be more evenly distributed, and were more stable in swift water. Each batteau could carry fifteen stacked hogsheads weighing close to 15,000 pounds.

Second, the batteaux were designed to move on shallow rivers with rapids, due to their flat bottom and pointed ends. The batteaux were steered with an oar, rather than a rudder, to allow them to be maneuvered in areas of still water. In addition to the "thole pins" that held the oar in place and allowed the batteaux to be rowed, they also could be poled in shallow water. Many bateaux had masts on which a square sail could be rigged. Since the bateaux had flat bottoms, the addition of a sail could still greatly lessen the amount of work to move them.

Lastly, batteaux did not require an experienced crew. Any man with a strong back could be employed. In private trade, this meant that wages could be kept fairly low.

Tobacco Boat (Batteau)
From Tatham, William, Essay on the Culture and
Commerce of Tobacco, London, 1800 Special
Collections, John D. Rockefeller, Jr. Library,
The Colonial Williamsburg Foundation

The first reference to the James River batteau is found in Jefferson's Memorandum Books: Accounts, with Legal Records and Miscellany, 1767-1826. On April 29, the Rucker brothers officially launched their James River batteau, and Thomas Jefferson was there to witness it. Thomas Jefferson recorded the purchase of one of these batteaux, stating, "Apr. 29, Rucker's battoe is 50. f. long. 4.f. wide in the bottom & 6.f. at top, she carries 11. hhds & draws 13 ½ l. water." [79] (translated: April 29, Rucker's batteau is fifty feet long, four feet wide in the bottom, and 6 feet at top, she carries 11 hogshead and draws 13 ½ litres of water.)

Besides tobacco, wheat, and flour, the batteaux owners also loaded them with farm products from the Virginia Valley. At the warehouse, three watermen, usually slave labor, rolled up to fifteen hogsheads directly on board each batteau, and carried the goods down the Fluvanna River, which became the James River at the town of Columbia, and was then transported on to Richmond to be sold. One man steered from the stern with a long oar-like sweep, while the remaining two pushed away from any visible boulders.

Due to weight, tobacco and flour shipments to Richmond were often delayed during times of drought, until there was enough water on the river to cover shallow areas. The journey downriver usually took between three to five days. The batteaux returned from Richmond with French and English imports such as furniture, dishes, and clothing, to stock the factor stores. The trip upriver, fighting the current, could take as long as ten days. (Visit smuseum@avenue.org for James River Batteau Festival)

Chapter XXXII:
August 1774

Coping with the recent family deaths, my extensive law practice, the inherited estate issues, overseeing the Shadwell interest, and the ongoing design and construction at Monticello, has put a great deal of pressure on me. After giving it much thought and deliberation, I recently decided to retire from my law practice, and have turned over all my unfinished cases to Edmund Randolph. I am torn between family and country, but will now have more freedom and occasion to engage in public office. First and foremost, I am a Virginian, and my allegiance is to the land that my father and forefathers labored over, for I believe that it is my responsibility and an honor to serve the country that I dearly love.

Construction started at Monticello in the beginning of 1769, and would eventually become a continual work in progress throughout Thomas Jefferson's later retirement years. The house that he, Martha, and their two young daughters were living in by 1774 was not the familiar home we currently see at Monticello today. While living in Paris between 1784 and 1789, Thomas Jefferson observed a new style of domestic architecture that was more elegant and less classical in form, and began to think about remodeling and enlarging Monticello. Demolition of the upper floors and the northeast front of the house began in1796, and all remodeling and enlargements were completed by 1809. When you visit Monticello today and stand on the north piazza, you will notice much of the original brickwork from the first floor incorporated in the southwest side of the house.

> *I have also been extremely preoccupied with the current events involving the Intolerable Acts passed by the British Parliament earlier this year in response to the Boston Tea Party of December 16th. These acts ignited outrage and resistance throughout the colonies, as we viewed them as arbitrary violations of our rights. I am planning to attend the First Continental Congress meeting on the 5th of September in Philadelphia, to show my opposition along with the other members, and to assist in coordinating a protest against Parliament's authority over our thirteen colonies.*

In retribution for the Boston Tea Party, an offense committed by the Boston colonists against the royal authority, the British Prime Minister, Lord North, began passing a series of five laws in the spring of 1774, dubbed the Coercive or Intolerable Acts, to punish the city of Boston. They were as follows:

- The Boston Port Act, passed on March 30, 1774, which was a direct action against the city for the previous December's "tea party." As a result of the protest, Parliament closed the port of Boston to all shipping until full restitution was made to the East India Company for the loss of their investment, as well as to the King for the loss of tea and tax revenue. Many Bostonians loudly protested that the act punished the entire city rather than the few who were responsible for the tea party. As supplies in the city dwindled, other sympathetic colonies began sending relief to the blockaded city.

- The Massachusetts Government Act, enacted on May 20, 1774, was designed to increase royal control over the Massachusetts's governing process. Annulling the colony's charter, the act stipulated that its executive council would no longer be democratically elected, and instead, its members would be appointed by the King. Also, many colonial offices that were previously elected officials would, henceforth, be appointed by the Royal Governor. Also, only one town meeting a year, across the colony, was permitted unless approved by the Governor.

- The Administration of Justice Act, which was also passed on May 20, 1774, stated that royal officials charged with criminal acts while fulfilling their duties, could request a change of venue to another colony, or to Great Britain. While the act allowed travel expenses to be paid to witnesses, few colonists could afford to leave work to testify at a trial. Dubbed the "Murder Act" by some, it was felt that it allowed royal officials to act with impunity, while escaping justice.

- The Quartering Act was a revision of the 1765 Quartering Act, and was largely ignored by colonial governing bodies. The 1774 Quartering Act expanded the types of buildings in which royal officials/soldiers could be provided with board and lodging, and removed the requirement that they be provided with provisions. Typically, soldiers were first to be placed in existing barracks and public houses, but thereafter, could be housed in inns, empty building, barns, and other unoccupied structures.

- The Quebec Act, though it did not have a direct effect on the thirteen colonies, was considered part of the Intolerable Acts by the colonists, and was intended to ensure the loyalty of the King's Canadian subjects. The act greatly enlarged Quebec's borders and allowed the free practice of the Catholic faith. Among the land transferred to Quebec was much of the Ohio country, which had been promised to several colonies through their charters, and to which many had already laid claim. In addition to the angered land speculators losing their claims, many others were fearful about the spread of Catholicism from Canada to America.

On July 25, 1774, I was elected to the First Virginia Convention of Delegates. Prior to the session, I had drafted a document as a set of instructions for the Virginia delegates, and planned to introduce it, myself, at the meeting in Williamsburg. In this document, I accused King George III of imposing illegal control over Virginia's political decisions, and I argued that the British Parliament had no right to govern the colonies, which, I claimed, had been independent since their founding.

Unfortunately, "I set out for Williamsburg some days before our meeting, but was taken ill of a dysentery on the road, and was unable to proceed. I sent on, therefore, to Williamsburg, two copies of my draught, the one under cover to Peyton Randolph, who I knew would be in the chair of the convention, the other to Patrick Henry. Whether Mr. Henry disapproved the ground taken, or was too lazy to read it (for he was the laziest man in reading I ever knew) I never learned; but he communicated it to nobody. Peyton Randolph informed the convention he had received such a paper from a member, prevented by sickness from offering it in his place, and he laid it on the table for perusal. It was read generally by the members, approved by many, though thought too bold for the present state of things."[80]

Peyton Randolph read the draft to an assembly of notable Virginia patriots gathered in his home on Market Square. Unfortunately, when presented to the House of Burgesses, they considered the draft too radical for official endorsement, and consequently, they adopted a more moderate position than the one Thomas Jefferson articulated.

But, a group of Jefferson's friends in Williamsburg persuaded the widow, Clementina Rind, at the Printing Office on Duke of Gloucester Street, to issue the draft as a pamphlet, and she agreed. It was entitled *A Summary View of the Rights of British America*, and was published the first week of August 1774, detailing the events that would eventually lead to the rift between Britain and the colonies. This would be the first of many important documents that Thomas Jefferson would write.

The pamphlet played a part in shaping the course of American self-rule. It was reprinted and circulated in Philadelphia, New York, and London, and helped to establish Jefferson's reputation as a proponent of change, a skillful political writer, and an independence-favoring radical. In 1776, delegate John Adams of Massachusetts said that the Summary View gave Jefferson "the reputation of masterly pen" among Congressional delegates, and won, for Jefferson, the assignment of drafting the Declaration of Independence.

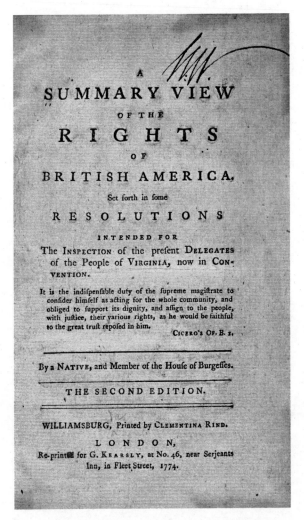

A

SUMMARY VIEW

OF THE

RIGHTS

OF

BRITISH AMERICA,

Set forth in some

RESOLUTIONS

INTENDED FOR

The INSPECTION of the present DELEGATES of the People of VIRGINIA, now in CONVENTION.

It is the indispensable duty of the supreme magistrate to consider himself as acting for the whole community, and obliged to support its dignity, and assign to the people, with justice, their various rights, as he would be faithful to the great trust reposed in him.

CICERO'S OF. B. 1.

By a NATIVE, and Member of the House of Burgesses.

THE SECOND EDITION.

WILLIAMSBURG, Printed by CLEMENTINA RIND.

LONDON,

Re-printed for G. KEARSLY, at No. 46, near Serjeants Inn, in Fleet Street, 1774.

Title page of Summary View of the Rights
of British America by Thomas Jefferson
Printed by Clementina Rind, 1774.
Special Collections, John D. Rockefeller, Jr. Library,
The Colonial Williamsburg Foundation

The Ludwell-Paradise House is a two-story Georgian style, brick home on the north side of Duke of Gloucester Street. It was originally built as a town-house by wealthy planter and member of the Governor's Council, Philip Ludwell III, around 1755. Philip III's second daughter, Lucy, inherited the house, but she lived most of her life in London with her husband, John Paradise, and rented the Williamsburg home. The first tenants were Joseph and Mary Pullet. The second tenants were William and Clementina Rind, who arrived with their four children from Annapolis, Maryland, in late 1765, after accepting an invitation from a group of Virginians, including Thomas Jefferson, to publish a "free paper" in Williamsburg.

The Ludwell-Paradise House
The Colonial Williamsburg Foundation

The first issue of Rind's *Virginia Gazette* appeared on May 16, 1766. Their newspaper and bookshop operated out of the present Ludwell-Paradise House on Duke of Gloucester Street. Following the death of William Rind in August 1773, the widow Clementina, now with five children to support, became the first woman printer for the colony, with assistance from a kinsman, John Pinkney, an apprentice, a Negro slave, and a semiskilled artisan. She assumed the editorship and business management of the *Virginia Gazette* without missing a single issue.

Masthead of *Virginia Gazette.* Clementina
Rind edition, April 21,1774
Special Collections, John D. Rockefeller, Jr. Library,
The Colonial Williamsburg Foundation

As editor, Clementina was careful to preserve the integrity pledged in the gazette's motto: "*Open To All Parties, But Influenced By None.*" The paper began to assume its place as a literary journal, publishing not only reports of foreign and domestic affairs, shipping news, and advertisements but also essays, articles, and poems. She also included vignettes about the life of Europe's high society, rural England, and in the other colonies. Clementina's bid for public favor was so well received that she expanded her printing program.

In May 1774, the House of Burgesses appointed Clementina Rind as "public printer" in her own right, and it continued to give her company all the public business, in spite of competing bids from Purdie and Dixon, the publishers of the rival *Virginia Gazette*. In August of that year, at the age of only thirty-four, Clementina Rind became ill and found it difficult to collect payments. She died in Williamsburg a month later, and was likely buried beside her husband at the Bruton Parish Church cemetery.

By early August 1774, Thomas Jefferson had not only built a thriving law practice, but he was overseeing his Shadwell plantation interests, tending to his Monticello garden and the construction of his hilltop home, taking care of his wife and young family, and was becoming more politically involved in the events leading up to the American Revolution.

On August 11, 1774, Thomas Jefferson retired from his law practice before the General Court in Charlottesville. Initially, he had preferred to transfer his large caseload over to Attorney General, John Randolph, who also was in private practice. It is assumed that John Randolph felt that he was unable to handle Jefferson's considerable caseload, and convinced Jefferson that his son, Edmund, was qualified to do the work. Edmund Randolph was well trained by his father, had just been admitted to the Virginia bar, but had also just celebrated his twenty-first birthday. With some reservation regarding his age and inexperience, Thomas Jefferson agreed to transfer over his cases to Edmund Randolph, and would never appear in General Court again.

Delivered to the young and newly licensed Randolph were 253 unfinished cases, less the caveats that Thomas Jefferson kept for himself. The caveat was a relatively simple court procedure regarding land patent litigation that demanded minimum effort, had a relatively short life, and paid relatively well. They were heard in the governor's private council and not by the General Court. Not only did Thomas retain the caveats, but he also accepted new caveat cases throughout 1774, while at the same time, shunning other kinds of new business that continued to come his way.

The small amount of cases accepted and listed in his casebook in early 1774 corroborates the conclusion that Thomas Jefferson was preparing to retire, and had probably made this decision sometime in 1773.

Chapter XXXIII:
Health and Wellness

Thomas Jefferson understood the benefits of a proper diet, exercise, and the correlation between good health and one's quality of life. He often offered his advice in correspondences to his friends and family. Thomas Jefferson once wrote, "...health is worth more than learning"[81] which is a strong statement since Thomas Jefferson was such a staunch believer of the importance of one's responsibility to pursue knowledge. He wrote, "Exercise is necessary for my health, and health is the first of all objects. A strong body makes the mind strong. If the body is feeble, the mind will not be strong. The sovereign invigoration of the body is exercise, and of all the exercises walking is best."[82]

Thomas Jefferson suffered from short and long-term sicknesses, starting in his early twenties, such as the common cold, dysentery, and severe headaches. His debilitating headaches usually occurred in times of stress, and correlated with personal loss, personal conflict, or deeply buried anger or guilt. He was plagued with the discomforts of rheumatoid arthritis, which caused pain and stiffness in his joints and muscles, as well as sciatic conditions, and diabetes. He often experienced swelling in his legs, possibly due to a serious kidney disorder, and used to bathe and bandage them.

Thomas Jefferson faced the dangers of illness, but remained relatively free from serious health problems during his lifetime most likely because he practiced and valued health maintenance. Mr. Jefferson took steps that he believed would keep him healthy and fit, occasionally consulting his physician, but often preferred to rely on the recuperative powers of nature. Being in charge of safe guarding his own health, and that of his family's, was a responsibility that he took seriously. He was convinced of the body's ability to heal itself, and often refused radical treatments.

Thomas Jefferson was raised to believe that plants and herbs possessed natural healing properties, besides being a food source. He began his Monticello garden in 1770, and by his retirement years (1809-1826), it had grown into a 1,000-foot terraced garden. More than a dozen herbs were cultivated along with other plants that had medicinal properties in the extensive terraced gardens at Monticello. Thomas recorded exact details about the garden in his Garden Book, while listing all the expenses and notes on every plant in season. His library of books on horticulture began to grow, as he wanted his family to enjoy a life built upon sound health practices. Focusing these efforts, Thomas Jefferson developed a regime of health care and mental vivacity which also helped him suppress the memories of the deaths of loved ones, as well as keep death's clutches from his body.

Many of Thomas Jefferson's views on personal health and medicine were considered forward thinking in his time. While residing at the boarding house of Mrs. Mary House during a brief visit to Philadelphia in May of 1766, Thomas Jefferson agreed to be inoculated against small pox, which was new to the colonists and a very controversial procedure. He was, though, highly skeptical of physicians and medicine, and believed that the field of medicine, at that time, was grounded in theory and not in science. Too often physicians proved to be inept, and he feared them more than he respected them. The medical treatments were rudimentary and primitive, and most times they offered no relief or cure.

Various diseases plagued the early colonists, some of which were contagious and others not, but all were deadly. Mosquitos spread intermittent fever, commonly known as malaria. Slow fever, commonly known as typhoid, was caused by contaminated and stagnant drinking water, which infected the digestive system. In addition, rotten quinsy, commonly known as diphtheria, defined as an acute and highly contagious infection that attacks the throat, generally resulted in a quick death by heart failure or asphyxiation. Cholera, an infection of the small intestine, caused a large amount of watery diarrhea, eventually causing death. The viral infection small pox was contagious, and struck with an unrelenting finality. Bilious fever referred to any fever that exhibited the symptoms of nausea and strong diarrhea, in addition to an increase in internal body temperature. The colonists also suffered from inflammatory disorders, such as dysentery, that affected the intestine and especially the colon, which resulted in fever and severe diarrhea containing mucus and/or blood in the feces. If left untreated, dysentery was fatal.

These diseases today would not be life threatening, but in the 1700s, medicine was not well developed, and people were not knowledgeable of the causes and possible cures.

Chapter XXXIV: Refreshed

As the sun is beginning to set over Monticello, a ribbon of orange, pink, and lavender lay across the horizon indicating that Cucullin and I ought to continue our return home. This refreshing afternoon spent in solitude and reflection has left me with a welcomed peace in my soul. Curiously, my headache has disappeared, and ever faithfully, my rock and my fortress have provided me refuge. Patty must be holding supper and wondering what could possibly have detained me.

I long for a tankard of chilled cider, and trust that Isaac has prepared a hearty meat supper with a large portion of the Indian corn and garden peas that have recently come to table. After the cloth is removed, perhaps Patty will join me for a glass of our favorite French Madeira wine during dessert. She and Patsy enjoy the sweet watermelon from the garden, but I am looking forward to one of Queen's delicious cherry-filled pastries.

Before retiring:

- *attend to paperwork regarding the transition of law practice over to Edmund Randolph, as well as "charge Sam.*

> *Taliaferro 2 days waggoning to wit the 17th and 18th.*"[83]
>
> - *Check if letter has yet arrived from Mr. Cox regarding whether he was able to engage a carpenter to begin work next Year's day.*
>
> *Tomorrow:*
> - *Check on the vineyard's first plantings from the land brokered to Filipo Mazzei.* (See Appendix VII.)

Before closing his Commonplace Book, Thomas Jefferson continues to scribble notes on the back page, listing chores for the following day. He collects his things and packs them in the saddlebag. After unhitching Cucullin, he mounts and continues down the trail in the westerly direction of Monticello. Thomas Jefferson rides across the Rivanna at the ford, where he and Dabney crossed many times during their youth, and proceeds up the mountain with a cheerful temperament. Refreshed and relaxed, Thomas begins to sing one of his sister Jane's favorite hymns, *Love Divine, All Loves Excelling...*

> *"Love divine, all loves excelling,*
> *Joy of heaven to earth come down;*
> *Fix in us thy humble dwelling;*
> *All thy faithful mercies crown!*
> *Jesus, Thou art all compassion,*
> *Pure unbounded love Thou art;*
> *Visit us with Thy salvation;*
> *Enter every trembling heart.*
>
> *Breathe, O breathe Thy loving Spirit,*
> *Into every troubled breast!*

Let us all in Thee inherit;
Let us find that second rest.
Take away our bent to sinning;
Alpha and Omega be;
End of faith, as its Beginning,
Set our hearts at liberty.

Come, Almighty to deliver,
Let us all Thy life receive;
Suddenly return and never,
Never more Thy temples leave.
Thee we would be always blessing,
Serve Thee as Thy hosts above,
Pray and praise Thee without ceasing,
Glory in Thy perfect love.

Finish, then, Thy new creation;
Pure and spotless let us be.
Let us see Thy great salvation
Perfectly restored in Thee;
Changed from glory into glory,
Till in heaven we take our place,
Till we cast our crowns before Thee,
Lost in wonder, love, and praise.

The End

Peter Jefferson and Jane Randolph Jefferson Family Birth Dates and Cause of Deaths

Peter Jefferson: Born February 29, 1708. Died at Shadwell on August 17, 1757, after two-month illness, cause unknown, age forty-nine.

Jane Randolph Jefferson: Born February 9, 1720. Died at Shadwell on March 31, 1776, of apoplexy (stroke), age fifty-six.

Children:

Jane Jefferson: Born June 27, 1740. Died suddenly at Shadwell on October 1, 1765, cause unknown, age twenty-five.

Mary Jefferson Bollings: Born October 1, 1741. Died at Chestnut Grove in Chesterfield County, Virginia, January 1804 of bilious fever. Specific date unknown, age sixty-two.

Thomas Jefferson: Born April 23, 1743. Died at Monticello on July 4, 1826, from a combination of illnesses and conditions including uremia, severe diarrhea, and pneumonia, age eighty-three.

Elizabeth Jefferson: Born November 4, 1744. Died at Shadwell on February 22, 1774, found two days later drowned in Rivanna, age twenty-nine.

Martha Jefferson Carr: Born May 29, 1746. Died at Spring Forest, in Goochland County, in September 3, 1811, cause unknown, age sixty-five.

Peter Field Jefferson: Born October 16, 1748. Died at Tuckahoe, cause unknown, less than one year old.

Son: Born March 9, 1750. Died at Tuckahoe, at birth.

Lucy Jefferson Lewis: Born October 10, 1752. Died at Rocky Hill, near the present-day town of Smithland, Kentucky, in 1784. Specific date and cause of death unknown, age thirty-one.

Twin Anna Scott Jefferson Marks: Born October 1, 1755. Died at Monticello on July 8, 1828, cause of death unknown, age seventy-two.

Twin Randolph Jefferson: Born October 1, 1755. Died at Snowden on August 7, 1815, cause unknown, age sixty.

Chronology of
Events 1743-1774

1743 13 Apr. Born Shadwell, Goochland (now Albemarle) County, Virginia.

1757 17 Aug. Father, Peter Jefferson, died.

1760 25 Mch. Entered College of William & Mary at Williamsburg, Virginia.

1762 25 Apr. Left College of William & Mary and began reading law with George Wythe in Williamsburg.

1765 1 Oct. Favorite sister, Jane, died.

1766 May, June, July. Traveled to Annapolis, Philadelphia, and New York, and while in Philadelphia, he was inoculated against small pox by Dr. William Shippen.

1767 12 Feb. Recorded first legal case.

18 Aug. – 4 Sep. Traveled to Augusta, Bedford, Amherst, Orange, Culpeper, Frederick, and Fauquier County seats. First visit to Natural Bridge.

1768 15 May Contracted to level a 250 foot square for a dwelling at Monticello.

24 May – 21 June In Williamsburg.

27 Sep. – 6 Nov. In Williamsburg.

9 Dec. Elected to House of Burgesses.

1769 5 Apr. – 15 June In Williamsburg.

8-17 May General Assembly met a Williamsburg. Took seat in House of Burgesses.

18 May Signed non-importation association

21 Sep. Elected to House of Burgesses.

6 Oct. – 25 Dec. In Williamsburg.

(During the year 1769, construction of a small dwelling, later the south pavilion, had begun at Monticello.)

1770 1 Feb. Shadwell home site burned.

14 Apr. – 8 May In Williamsburg.

21 May – 28 June Assembly met in Williamsburg.

5-30 June In Williamsburg.

6 Oct. – 9 Nov. In Williamsburg.

26 Nov. Moved to south pavilion at Monticello.

10-16 Dec. In Williamsburg.

1771 8 Apr. – 13 May In Williamsburg.

9-20 June In Williamsburg.

11-20 July In Williamsburg; attended Assembly.

8 Oct. – 6 Nov. In Williamsburg.

29 Nov. Elected to House of Burgesses.

1772 1 Jan. Married Martha Wayles Skelton at The Forest.

10 Feb. – 12 Apr. Assembly met at Williamsburg.

9 Apr. – 11 June In Williamsburg.

27 Sept. Daughter Martha born.

11 Oct. – 2 Nov. In Williamsburg.

1773 4-13 Mch. Assembly met at Williamsburg.

4-c. 24 Mch. In Williamsburg.

9 Apr. – 8 May In Williamsburg.

6-11 June In Williamsburg.

11 June – 10 July At The Forest.

10 Oct. – 4 Dec. In Williamsburg.

1774 21-22 Feb. Earthquake at Monticello.

24 Feb. Sister Elizabeth died.

3 Apr. Second daughter Jane Randolph born.

18-24 Apr. In Williamsburg.

5-26 May Assembly met at Williamsburg.

c. 9-31 May In Williamsburg.

27 May Signed non-imp. Association

8-16 June In Williamsburg.

25 July Elected to 1st Va. Convention, but could not attend because of illness.

c. 8 Aug. "Summary View of Rights of British America" published.

Aug. Turned over Gen. Court practice to Edmund Randolph.

17 Aug. Recd. a letter from Mr. Cox in which he informs me he has engaged a carpenter for me to begin next Year's day.

Charge Sam. Taliaferro two days waggoning to wit the 17th & 18th

Chart of Virginia Counties 1761-1770

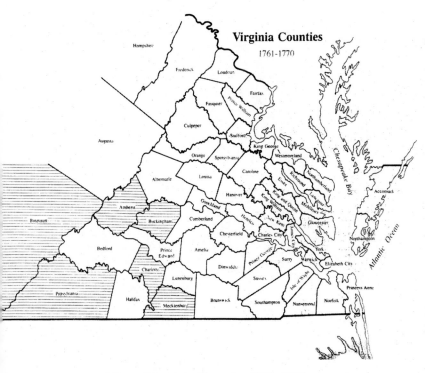

Map of Virginia Counties 1761-1770
Atlas of County Boundary Changes in Virginia
1634-1895, by Michael F. Doran.
The Albemarle-Charlottesville Historical Society

Thomas Jefferson's Landholdings in Albemarle County, Virginia, as of 1774

Fredericksville Parish:

1. Shadwell. 400 acres, inherited from Peter Jefferson.

2. Lego. 819 1/4 acres, purchased in 1774.

3. Pantops. inherited from Peter Jefferson

4. Limstone tract. 4 acres, purchased in 1771.

5. Pouncey's. 400 acres, inherited from Peter Jefferson.

Saint Anne's Parish:

6. Monticello. 1,000 acres, inherited from Peter Jefferson.

7. Tufton. 150 acres, inherited from Peter Jefferson.

8. Portobello. 150 acres, inherited from Peter Jefferson.

Bedford County:

9. Judith's Creek. 2,042 acres, inherited from John Wayles.

10. Poplar Forest. 5,619 acres, inherited from John Wayles.

Amherst County:

11. Part of Judith's Creek. 280 acres, inherited from John Wayles.

Cumberland County:

12. Willis Creek. 1,076 acres, inherited from John Wayles.

Goochland County:

13. Elk Hill. 307 acres, purchased in 1774.

14. Elk Island. 333 acres, to which Martha Jefferson had dower rights from her late husband Bathurst Skelton.

Rockbridge County:

15. Natural Bridge. 157 acres, patented on July 5, 1774.

Henrico County:

16. Four lots in town of Beverley, inherited from Peter Jefferson.

City of Richmond:

17. Part of a lot, purchased in 1774

After 1774, Thomas Jefferson would continue to acquire acreage in Albemarle County. In 1777, he purchased acreage surrounding the Pantops farm to total 819 1/2 acres, as well as purchase a 483-acre neighboring mountain tract that rises 400 feet above Monticello, known as Montalto.

Thomas Jefferson's landholdings in Albemarle County, alone, eventually totaled some 5,000 acres. To manage this vast estate, Jefferson divided the land into separate farms. The area surrounding his Monticello home constituted what he called the home farm, or Monticello Mountain. Outlying lands were divided into manageable parcels known as quarter farms and were run by resident overseers. Thomas Jefferson's quarter farms were Tufton, which was adjacent to Monticello, and Shadwell and Lego farms, both north of the Rivanna. Jefferson sought to further organize his farms by dividing them into agricultural fields of forty acres each.

After Thomas Jefferson's death in 1826, his daughter and heir, Martha Jefferson Randolph was compelled to sell Monticello and much of its contents, the surrounding farms, and most of its slaves to pay her father's debts. The Dispersal Sale, held in January 1827, scattered his possessions among members of his family, as well as numerous buyers, chiefly from Albemarle and neighboring counties. Since the Thomas Jefferson Memorial Foundation took title to Monticello in 1923, it has acquired a large amount of his possessions.

Currently, the landholdings of Thomas Jefferson now include approximately 2,500 of Jefferson's original 5,000 acres, of which more than 1,400 are held under protective easements, thanks to the Thomas Jefferson Foundation.

Thomas Jefferson's Legacy and Accomplishments from 1774–1826

Thomas Jefferson died at his beloved Monticello on July 4, 1826, the 50th anniversary of the signing of the Declaration of Independence. He was 83 years old.

The following people surrounded him at his bedside:

- Dr. Robley Dunglison, the twenty-seven-year-old English physician who treated him for migraine headaches, intestinal and urinary infections, and rheumatoid arthritis

- Thomas Jefferson Randolph, his grandson

- Nicholas Trist, the husband of Jefferson's granddaughter, Virginia Randolph

On the morning of July 3rd, Thomas Jefferson awoke from a nights rest, and remarked, "This is the Fourth of July," but it was only the third. He was fighting with every ounce of his being to live until the fourth. Dr. Robley Dunglison came in that morning to administer his medicine, laudanum, and Jefferson said,"Ah,

Doctor, are you still there?" Then he asked, "Is it the Fourth?" Dr. Dunglison answered, "It soon will be."

The night of July 3rd, Jefferson was partly delirious. At eleven o'clock in the morning of July 4th, his lips moved, and his grandson, Thomas Jefferson Randolph, son of Thomas Mann and Martha Jefferson-Randoph, applied a wet sponge to his mouth. Then Jefferson lost consciousness.

Death came two hours later at 12:50 p.m., on the Fourth of July, 1826, 50 years to the day, after the signing of the Declaration of Independence.

Thomas Jefferson's funeral, by his own request, was a simple and quiet affair, and performed by Reverend Frederick Hatch, rector of both the Middle Church in Cismont, and Christ Episcopal Church in Charlottesville. At five o'clock in the afternoon on the day after his death, his remains were carried by "servants, family and friends" to the Monticello graveyard, where he was interred under the great oak, next to his schoolmate, dearest friend, and brother-in-law Dabney Carr, fulfilling their childhood promise. Today, the great oak no longer stands.

Amongst all of Thomas Jefferson's achievements, he wished to be remembered for only three achievements in his public life. On his tombstone in the Monticello Cemetery, it reads that Thomas Jefferson was the "Author of the Declaration of American Independence, of the Statute of Virginia for Religious Freedom, and Father of the University of Virginia" and, as he requested, "not a word more...because by these, as testimonials that I have lived, I wish most to be remembered."

Thomas Jefferson had written his own epitaph, found in a drawer in his desk. Today, tourists who visit Monticello Cemetery, read the following inscription on the granite obelisk over his grave:

Here was Buried
THOMAS JEFFERSON
Author of the
Declaration
of
American Independence
of the
Statute of Virginia
for
Religious Freedom
and Father of the
University of Virginia

Besides being a devoted husband and father, Thomas Jefferson's illustrious accomplishments after August 1774 were as follows:

- 1775–Attends Second Continental Congress
- 1776–Drafts Declaration of Independence
- 1777–Serves in Virginia House of Delegates until 1779
- 1779–Elected Governor of Virginia
- 1782–Buries his beloved wife Martha
- 1783–Elected to Congress

- 1785–Appointed to succeed Benjamin Franklin as the Minister to France until 1789.

- 1789–Returns to United States from Paris.

- 1790–Appointed first US Secretary of State in George Washington's administration.

- 1793 to 1796–Retires briefly, spending time with family and on his farm at Monticello.

- 1796–Elected Vice President under John Adams

- 1801–Elected third President on thirty-sixth ballot in House of Representatives

- 1803–Commissions Lewis & Clark expedition. Concludes Louisiana Purchase.

- 1804–Re-elected President of the United States

- 1809–Retires to Monticello

- 1815–Sells personal library of 6,487 books to Library of Congress for $23,950.00.

- 1817–Conceives, plans, designs, supervises construction, and hires faculty for the University of Virginia.

- 1826 – Dies at age eighty-three, on July 4, the fiftieth anniversary of signing the Declaration of Independence.

Appendix I:

The Thomas Jefferson Foundation and Monticello

www.monticello.org

As a private, nonprofit organization, the Thomas Jefferson Foundation receives no regular federal, state, or local governmental support, and relies on the private support of donors to empower its capacity to preserve and educate. Philanthropy enables Monticello to serve as the premier institution dedicated to illuminating the physical, intellectual, and philosophical worlds of Jefferson.

The foundation is distinguished for its world-class library and academic center, its acquisition and protection of 2,500 acres of Jefferson's original 5,000-acre plantation, and its twenty-first-century visitor gateway and education center, welcoming nearly a half-million visitors annually. Since its founding in 1923, the Thomas Jefferson Foundation has been committed to its dual mission of preservation and education. Monticello was the center of Jefferson's world, and the Thomas Jefferson Foundation is dedicated to preserving Monticello and engaging a global audience in a dialogue with Jefferson's ideas.

The Colonial Williamsburg Foundation and Colonial Williamsburg

www.colonialwilliamsburg.com

The Colonial Williamsburg Foundation is the not-for-profit educational and cultural organization dedicated to the preservation, interpretation, and presentation of the restored 18th-century Revolutionary capital of Virginia. The foundation's purpose, in the words of the Board of Trustees, is "to re-create accurately the environment of the men and women of eighteenth-century Williamsburg, and to bring about such an understanding of their lives and times, that present and future generations may more vividly appreciate the contribution of these early Americans to the ideals and culture of our country."

Today, the Historic Area of Colonial Williamsburg embraces the heart of the old city, and includes eighteenth and early nineteenth-century structures within and near the historic area. Also, acres of colorful gardens and greens have been re-created, using chiefly plants known to the eighteenth-century colonists.

Appendix II:
Charlottesville, Virginia

www.cvillechamber.com

Charlottesville, Virginia, was founded by an Act of the Assembly, as the Albemarle County seat in 1762 with Dr. Thomas Walker, of Castle Hill, as Trustee. The Virginia General Assembly conveyed the future city land to Dr. Walker to be sold for the benefit of Albemarle County.

Charlotte Sophia, Duchess of Mecklenburg-Strelitz, married King George III on September 8, 1761, in St. James Palace, London; four months after Chief Ostenaco, Chief Cumnacatogue, and Chief Pouting Pigeon visited King George III in London. As King George's Queen consort, Charlotte Sophia was known as Queen Charlotte. Charlottesville was, hence, named after her in 1762.

In 2004, in a comprehensive analysis of nearly 400 metropolitan areas, the Greater Charlottesville community was ranked as "America's Best Place to Live" in Frommer's landmark publication Cities Ranked & Rated.

Here are a few other high-ranking recognitions for Charlottesville:

- Money: Best Places to Live
- Arts & Entertainment TV: One of the Best Places to Live in America
- Relocate America: Best Place to Relocate
- Forbes: Best Small Places To Do Business
- Forbes: Best Small Market for Business by Forbes
- Forbes/Milken Institute: Best Small Places for Business & Career
- Best City for Living and Launching a Business by Fortune & Money
- Money: 100 Best Places to Live
- Modern Maturity: Most Alive Places to Live
- Readers' Digest: Top Ten Places in the Country to Raise a Family
- Number One City for Retirement–Kiplinger.com
- Travel 50 & Beyond: Top Ten Great Places to Retire
- Kiplinger: Top Places to Retire
- Kiplinger: 4th Best Place to Live
- Forbes: 11th Best Town to Find a Job
- 18th Safest Mid-Sized Cities in the Country, Farmers Insurance
- Healthiest Place to Live–Men's Journal

- Men's Journal: #3 Healthiest Small City to Live in America
- American Health: Top Ten Healthiest Cities for Women
- AARP: Top 10 Healthiest Places to Retire
- Best Places to Retire, Black Enterprise
- Forbes: Best Small Market for Business by Forbes
- National Trust for Historic Preservation, Distinctive Destination
- Southern Business & Development Magazine: #1 on the list of 10 "Really Cool Small Southern
- Markets" Top "Brainiest" Metropolitan Areas– The Atlantic
- Outside: One of Seven Dream Towns That Have it All, Best Town to Live
- Kiplinger's Personal Finance: #2 Healthiest Place to Live in America
- Golf Digest: Best Retirement City for Golfers
- Tennis: Best Tennis Town
- Outside: Best Trail Running
- Cottage Living: Great Place to Live
- Blue Ridge: Top Five Green Cities
- Southern Business & Development: Top "Really Cool Small Southern Market"
- Business Journals–Best Places to Work

Appendix III: Recipes

Henry Wetherburn's Arrack Punch (contains no alcohol)

Ingredients for "punch bowl" serving:
- 1 large punch bowl
- 1/2 gallon of lime Sherbert
- 1 litre of Ginger Ale
- 1 small can of pineapple rings
- 6 round thin slices of lime (or other citrus: oranges or lemon)
- 1/4 tsp. of ground nutmeg

Run warm tap water, not hot, over the sherbert container to loosen sherbert. In a large punch bowl, place the contents of container of sherbert up side down in punch bowl. Pour Ginger Ale around sherbert. Float pineapple rings and lime (or other citrus) slices. Sprinkle nutmeg over sherbert.

Henry Wetherburn's Arrack Punch (contains alcohol)

(Warning: You must be of legal age to consume alcohol)

Ingredients for "per glass" serving:
    2 Tbsp. (or 1 ounce) Turbinado (raw) sugar
    2 Tbsp. (or 1 ounce) hot water
    3/4 ounces of Cognac
    3/4 ounces of Antigua Rum
    Juice from 2 squeezed lime slices
    2 ounces (a splash) of cold water
    Glass of ice
    Sprinkle of ground nutmeg
    Slice of lime for garnish

In a shaker: Dissolve Turbinado sugar in hot water. Add Cognac, rum, juice from 2 squeezed lime slices, and 2 ounces of cold water (a splash). Pour over a glass of ice, and garnish with grated nutmeg and a slice of lime. To serve in a punch bowl: multiply recipe for as many people as you want, and pour over a glass of ice. Garnish each glass with grated nutmeg and a slice of lime.

Ginger Cakes (Ginger Bread Cookies 50-60 cookies)

Ingredients:

- 1 cup sugar
- 2 teaspoons ginger
- 1 teaspoon nutmeg
- 1 teaspoon cinnamon
- 1/2 teaspoon salt
- 1 1/2 teaspoons baking soda
- 1 cup margarine (melted)
- 1/2 cup evaporated milk
- 1 cup unsulfured molasses
- 3/4 teaspoons vanilla extract (optional)
- 3/4 teaspoons lemon extract (optional)
- 4 cups stone-ground or unbleached flour (un-sifted)

Combine the sugar, ginger, nutmeg, cinnamon, salt, and baking soda. Mix well. Add the melted margarine, evaporated milk, and molasses. Add the extracts if desired. Mix well. Add the flour 1 cup at a time, stirring constantly. The dough should be stiff enough to handle without sticking to fingers. Knead the dough for a smoother texture. Add up to 1/2 cup additional flour if necessary to prevent sticking. When the dough is smooth, roll it out 1/4 inch thick on a floured surface and cut it into cookies. Bake on floured or greased cookie sheets in a preheated 375 degrees F. oven for 10-12 minutes. The cookies are done if they spring back when touched.

Queen's Cake

Ingredients:
- 1 cup butter
- 1 cup sugar
- 5 eggs
- 1 teaspoon lemon extract
- 1 teaspoon orange extract
- 2 cups plus 1 tablespoon all-purpose flour
- 1/2 teaspoon baking powder
- 1/2 teaspoon cinnamon
- 2 cups currants

All of the ingredients should be at room temperature. Grease well and lightly flour a 9 1/4 x 5 1/4 inch loaf pan. Cream the butter and sugar. Add the eggs, 1 at a time, beating well after each addition. Add the lemon and orange extracts. Sift 2 cups of flour with the baking powder and cinnamon. Gradually add the flour mixture to the egg mixture. Dust the currants with the remaining 1 tablespoon of flour so they do not sink to the bottom of the mixture. Fold the currants into the mixture. Bake in a preheated 325-degree F oven for 1 hour and 20 minutes, or until done. Cool in the pan for 10 minutes before turning out onto a rack. Slice thinly.

Oatmeal Cakes
(Oatmeal Cookies 4 dozen)

Ingredients:
- 1 cup shortening
- 1 cup sugar
- 2 eggs
- ½ cup molasses
- ¼ cup milk
- 2 cups all-purpose flour
- ½ teaspoon salt
- ½ teaspoon baking soda
- 2 teaspoons cinnamon
- 1 teaspoon cloves
- 2 cups quick-cooking oats
- ½ cup raisins or currants (optional)

Cream the shortening and sugar. Add the eggs, molasses, and mild. Beat well. Sift the flour, salt, baking soda, cinnamon, and cloves together and add to the creamed mixture along with the quick-cooking oats. Add the raisins or currants if desired. Drop the mixture by heaping-teaspoon full onto ungreased cookie sheets. Bake in a preheated 350 degree F. oven for 8 to 10 minutes or until brown, but still soft.

Shrewsbury Cakes
(Sugar Cookies 3 dozen)

Ingredients:
- ¼ cup unsalted butter
- ¼ cup shortening
- 1 cup sugar
- 1 ½ teaspoons grated orange peel
- 1 teaspoon vanilla extract
- 1 egg
- 3 tablespoons mild
- 2 cups sifted all-purpose flour
- 1 teaspoon salt
- 2 teaspoons cream of tartar

Cream the butter, shortening, and sugar. Add the orange peel and vanilla extract. Add the egg and milk. Sift the flour, baking soda, salt, and cream of tartar and add to the creamed mixture. Mix well. Roll into 1-inch balls and roll the balls in sugar. Arrange the balls 1 ½ inches apart on ungreased cookie sheets. Flatten the balls gently with a small glass. Bake in a preheated 350-degree F oven for 8 to 10 minutes, or until very light golden brown.

Appendix IV:
Shadwell Today

Today, Shadwell is owned by the Thomas Jefferson Foundation, and is not open to the general public. Wooden fencing still lines the driveway of the entrance to the Shadwell property located off of Virginia State Route 250 East in Charlottesville, Virginia, and is marked with the Virginia Historical Highway Marker W-202.

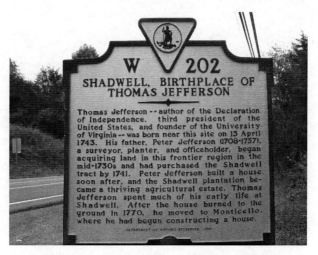

W-202 Shadwell–Birthplace of Thomas Jefferson
Author's personal photo library Courtesy of the Virginia
Department of Historic Resources, Richmond, Virginia

The Shadwell property, once a thriving tobacco plantation, has been given over to cattle grazing.

A granite stone marker stands at the alleged home site which signifies Thomas Jefferson's birth place. It reads as follows:

HERE WAS BORN

THOMAS JEFFERSON
APRIL 13, 1743

———

LOVER OF LIBERTY

Thomas Jefferson Birth Marker at Shadwell
Author's personal photo library Courtesy of the
Monticello/Thomas Jefferson Foundation, Inc.

Appendix V:
Blenheim Vineyards,
Charlottesville, Virginia

www.blenheimvineyards.com

View of Blenheim Vineyards
Courtesy of Jack Looney, Photographer

Blenheim Vineyards is located twenty minutes south-east of Charlottesville, and just eight miles from Monticello. With three vineyard sites growing seven varieties, the goal at Blenheim Vineyards is to make high quality wines that reflect the climate, soil, and beauty of the surrounding piedmont landscape. The winery offers a variety of red wines, white wines, and rosé. Tastings are available daily. The property was nominated to the Virginia Landmarks Register on December 16, 1975, and to the National Register of Historic Places on May 17, 1976.

Appendix VI:
The Natural Bridge,
Natural Bridge, Virginia

www.naturalbridgeva.com

Today, Natural Bridge is still one of our nation's most visited natural wonders. Thomas Jefferson's rock bridge remains, as does the legend of the Monacan Indians who discovered it, deeming it the "Bridge of God". Jefferson's vision transpired over time, and his two-room cabin eventually grew into a hotel. Since 1927, the bridge has also captivated visitors at night during the "Drama of Creation", when colorful lights dance across the rock, accompanied by Biblical narration, music, the light of the moon, and soothing sounds of Cedar Creek.

The Natural Bridge of Virginia, Natural Wonder & Historic Landmark, is open year round. For lodging, tours information and tickets, contact 1-800-533-1410, or email info@naturalbridgeva.com.

Appendix VII:
Philip (Filipo/Filippo) Mazzei and Jefferson Vineyards, Charlottesville, Virginia

www.jeffersonvineyards.com

Filippo Mazzei was born December 25, 1730, in Poggio a Caiano, in the Province of Prato, the Tuscany region of Italy. He studied medicine in Florence, and practiced in Italy and the Middle East for several years before moving to London to take up a career as a wine merchant in 1754.

While working in London as a wine importer and exporter, Mazzei met and befriended two Americans, Benjamin Franklin, commercial representative from Pennsylvania, and Thomas Adams, businessman and legislative representative for Augusta County, Virginia. Mazzei talked to Franklin about his idea of importing Tuscan wine and olive trees to the New World. Benjamin Franklin persuaded Mazzei to expand his agricultural business in Virginia, where the climate, both physical and ideological, would be more congenial to Mazzei's political and philosophical beliefs. Under the sponsorship and financial backing of Thomas Adams, Mazzei agreed to come to Virginia to establish a plantation for the production of silk, olives, and vineyards.

Mazzei prepared for his trip with enthusiasm. Before leaving Italy, Mazzei carefully selected and brought with him ten Tuscan farmers, indentured servants who were experienced in the culture of vines and olive trees, as well as the production of silk.

On September 2, 1773, Filippo Mazzei sailed for America from Livorno, Italy, in the chartered frigate, *The Triumph*, along with his wife-to-be, Maria Martin and her daughter, a full load of cuttings, seeds, tools, silkworms, a tailor, and the ten grape farmer/winemakers. They arrived in late November at a port on the James River, Trebell's Landing & Burwell's Ferry, just four miles from Williamsburg, Virginia.

As Mazzei's fame quickly spread among the gentlemen farmers of Virginia, Thomas Adams introduced Mazzei to Thomas Jefferson, who shared his extensive knowledge of Italian wines, cheeses, and olive trees.

Mazzei planned to settle on Thomas Adams' 4000-acre plantation in Augusta County, but once he discovered that the land was divided into separate tracts, he did not accept it. Mazzei left his workmen in Williamsburg to go westward to search for a site suitable for farming grapes and olive trees.

While traveling through Albemarle County, he stopped to visit Thomas Jefferson, who was pleased to invite the Italian visitor to rest at Monticello. At the time, Thomas Jefferson was engaged in agricultural experimentation, and was delighted to talk shop with his personable visitor.

The next morning, Jefferson took Mazzei for a tour of his hilltop, as well as to a 193-acre plantation that he owned, located at the southern base of Monticello. After Thomas Jefferson elaborated to Mazzei about the quality of Albemarle's rich, red clay soil, he invited Mazzei to become a neighbor, and successfully persuaded him to establish a vineyard. Thomas Jefferson then brokered the sale of his land to Mazzei, who upon acceptance of Jefferson's offer, immediately summoned his imported laborers from Williamsburg.

Mazzei announced his proposal to form a company/partnership for the commercial production and sale of wine from the vineyards at his farm, "Colle" (Italian for "hill"). Thanks to the efforts of Thomas Jefferson, he had no trouble finding subscribers. A committee was formed to oversee all the matters relating to the affairs of the company. The committee members consisted of his Excellency Earl Dunmore, the Honorable; John Page of Rosewell, Esqr., the Honorable; Peyton Randolph, Esqr.; Robert C. Nicholas; Thomas Nelson, Junr.; John Blair; and Wilson Miles Cary and James McClurg, Esqrs..

Thomas Jefferson induced his friends and neighbors to invest in the Wine Company, and was instrumental in procuring their subscriptions. Most of the original subscribers, eager to participate in the production and encouragement of viniculture in Virginia, bought one share at £50 sterling per share, including Thomas Jefferson, while Filippo Mazzei purchased four shares.

The list of the original subscriber names, and the number of shares they purchased, are noted in Thomas Jefferson's *Fee Book & Miscellaneous Accounts*. They are as follows:

Dunmore, four shares.

Petyon Randolph, £50.Stel:

R.C. Nicholas, two shares.

Thos. Adams, one share.

James Donald, one share.

G Mason, one share.

Go: Washington, one share.

John Page, one share

John Page of Rosewell one share

Th: Jefferson one share,

John Banister one share

John Blair one share

Theo: Bland Jr. one share

John Tayloe one share

Archbald Cary one share

Wilson Miles Carey one share

Jams. Parke Farley one share

John Parke Custis.

Joseph Scott, & Ths. Pleasants one share

Robert Pleasants, one share, on condition that he may withdraw his subscription in case, that any slaves should be purchased on account of the Company.

Benja. Harrison, Brandon, one share

Thomas M. Randolph, one share.

James McClurg one share.

Peter Randoph, one share.

Thos. Nelson jr., one share.

Richd. & Everard Meade one share

Chars. Carter Junr. one Share

Daniel L. Hilton one share

William Murray one share.

Rayland Randolph one share

Allen Cocke one share

Philip Mazzei four shares

Mann Page Junr, & Hugh Nelson one share

John Tabb one share

Richard Randolph one share

Thomas Jefferson arranged for the monies to be paid to Mazzei in the city of Williamsburg, "¼ to be paid on or before the first day of November 1774, and one other ¼ part at the end of every six months after, until the whole be paid."[84]

Mazzei wasted no time in organizing his wine company, and started his experimental plantation in full view of Monticello, and under the watchful eye of his friend and neighbor, Thomas Jefferson.

The first plantings of the European vinifera varieties were established in the early spring of 1774. In May of that year, the project failed when a severe frost ruined the vines that had been so carefully planted. Much to his disappointment, Mazzei still felt that Virginia's soil and climate were "better calculated" for wine production than any other area.

Philip Mazzei and Thomas Jefferson
by Artist Shannon Stirnweis
Courtesy of the Unicover Corporation,
Cheyenne, Wyoming

Mazzei's and Jefferson's fruitful commercial partnership bloomed into an intellectual rapport that lasted some 40 years. As a result of their friendship, the town of Charlottesville, Virginia, and the municipal territory of Poggio a Caiano, Italy, became rooted together as a sisterhood. The multi-dimensional friendship between Mazzei and Jefferson inspired Poggio and Charlottesville to officially link the two cities in 1977, in commemoration of the bicentennial celebration of the American Revolution.

Besides all Thomas Jefferson's efforts noted above, he also assisted Mazzei as legal counsel by writing the "Plan of Philip Mazzei's Agricultural Company" which were the proposals for forming the "Company or Partnership, for the Purpose of raising and making Wine, Oil, agruminous Plants and Silk."[85]

The site of Filippo Mazzei's home, "Colle", originally built in 1774 by workers engaged in building Monticello, was recognized by the Commonwealth of Virginia, in 1928, with a state historical marker. Today, "Colle" is part of the Jefferson Vineyards estate, one of the more established wineries and vineyards in Virginia.

The winery at Jefferson Vineyards has been in operation since the early 1980's, and has been home to a number of very talented wine makers and leaders in the Virginia wine industry. It was named after Thomas Jefferson due to Jefferson persuasively inducing Mazzei to settle near Monticello, his instrumental involvement in the development of Mazzei's experimental vineyard/wine company, and their unshakeable 40-year friendship. It is a modest farm winery which produces between 6,000 and 8,000 cases of wine per year at the southern base of Monticello. Jefferson Vineyards offers premiere wines of superior quality, and takes great pride in holding fast to the Jeffersonian values of winemaking in Virginia.

Jayne D'Alessandro-Cox

Jefferson Vineyards
Courtesy of Jefferson Vineyards, Charlottesville, Virginia

References

Image Sources

Crop of Thomas Jefferson signature from engraving of Thomas Jefferson in Duyckinck, Every A., National Portrait Gallery of Eminent Americans...New York: Johnson, Fry & Company, 1860, Volume I. Image # D2004-COPY-1013-2014. Special Collections, John D. Rockefeller, Jr. Library, The Colonial Williamsburg Foundation.

Miniature Portrait of Thomas Jefferson by John Trumbull, circa 1788. Oil on mahogany, 4 1/2 x 3 1/4 in. (11.4 x 8.3 cm). Bequest of Cornelia Cruger, 1923, (24.19.1). Image copyright © The Metropolitan Museum of Art, New York. Image source: Art Resource, NY.

Colonial Williamsburg historical interpreter, Bill Barker, portrays Thomas Jefferson on horseback. Image #94-1991. The Colonial Williamsburg Foundation.

Greenstone Outcrop at Shadwell, Albemarle County, Virginia. Author's personal photo library, courtesy of the Thomas Jefferson Foundation at Monticello.

Tobacco Field. Image # D2009-BTL-0114-1045. The Colonial Williamsburg Foundation.

Factor Store Certificate/Tobacco Warehouse Receipt, June 16, 1777. Image # 1965-CK-3297. Special Collections, John D. Rockefeller, Jr. Library, The Colonial Williamsburg Foundation.

James Mills Scottish Factor Store or "Old Tobacco Warehouse," waterfront on the Rappahonnock River, Urbanna, Virginia. Courtesy of Dave Lipscombe, L! Marketing & Design

West View of Tuckahoe House. Author's personal photo library, courtesy of the Tuckahoe Plantation, Richmond, Virginia.

Rosewell Mansion, circa 1875. Courtesy of The Valentine Richmond History Center, Richmond, Virginia.

Shirley Plantation on the James River. Courtesy of Shirley Plantation, Charles City, Virginia.

Map of Transatlantic Voyage, circa 1700. Tate Publishing Illustration Department.

House of Burgesses, Capitol Building, Williamsburg. Reenactment of Patrick Henry's "Caesar-Brutus" speech and his defiant resolutions opposing the Stamp Act, May 15, 1776. Image # 95-224. The Colonial Williamsburg Foundation.

Castle Hill, home of Dr. Thomas Walker. Sketch of original clapboard colonial residence, built 1765. The Albemarle Charlottesville Historical Society, Charlottesville, Virginia.

Tuckahoe Schoolhouse. Author's personal photo library, courtesy of the Tuckahoe Plantation, Richmond, Virginia.

Eighteenth century Gristmill. Tate Publishing Illustration Department.

The Rivanna at Shadwell. Author's personal photo library.

Cherokee Chief Ostenaco. Image #08958100 (also called Chief Outassete, Outacite, or Austenaco)

National Anthropological Archives, Smithsonian Institution [item id].

The Three Cherokees, published by George Bickham, London, ca. 1765, black and white line engraving, accession # 1958-484. Image # TC2001-357. Special Collections, John D. Rockefeller, Jr. Library, The Colonial Williamsburg Foundation.

Reverend James Maury Grave and Original Site of Middle Church. Grace Episcopal Church, Walker's Parish, in background. Author's personal photo library. Courtesy of Grace Episcopal Church Vestry, Jefferson Highway, Cismont, Virginia.

Sir Christopher Wren Building. Print of College of William & Mary, lithograph by Crump after a painting by Thomas Millington, ca. 1850, accession # 1975-264. Image #KC1976-105. The Colonial Williamsburg Foundation. Museum Purchase.

The Bruton Parish Church. Image # D2009-BTL-0219-1004. The Colonial Williamsburg Foundation. Gift of Vestry of Bruton Parish Church.

Raleigh Tavern. Image # 93-740. The Colonial Williamsburg Foundation.

Thomas Jefferson's Tuition Entry. College of William and Mary Office of the Bursar Records, Special Collection Research Center, Earl Gregg Swem

Library, The College of William and Mary, Williamsburg, Virginia. Entry 1762-1763.

Dr. William Small, Courtesy of The Muscarelle Museum of Art at The College of William & Mary in Virginia

Governor's Palace, residence of the king's deputy. Image # 2000-337. The Colonial Williamsburg Foundation.

Market Square Tavern. Image # 93-606. The Colonial Williamsburg Foundation.

Wythe House Rear Entrance. Image # 91-781. The Colonial Williamsburg Foundation.

George Wythe, Esq., by William H. Crossman, New York, 1927, accession # 1938-226. Image # KC13e. The Colonial Williamsburg Foundation.

General Court Room, Capitol Building. Image # 88-705. The Colonial Williamsburg Foundation.

Snowden Property at Horseshoe Bend on James River, Virginia. Burgess Collection. The Scottsville Museum, Scottsville, Virginia. CDB3Roll2Neg3A.

Portraits of King George III and Queen Charlotte by Studio of Allan Ramsay, London, 1770, oil on canvas, accession # 1936-376. Image # DS1993-598 and TC1994-17. The Colonial Williamsburg Foundation. Museum Purchase.

Snowden House built c. 1857, Scott's Landing, Virginia. Burgess Collection. The Scottsville Museum, Scottsville, Virginia. CDB3RollTenNeg16A.

General Courthouse (1803), Charlottesville, Virginia. Author's Personal Photo Library.

Natural Bridge, Natural Bridge, Virginia. Image # K1998-DMD-37,13s. The Colonial Williamsburg Foundation.

Grace Episcopal Church, Walker's Parish. Author's personal photo library. Courtesy of Grace Episcopal Church Vestry, Jefferson Highway, Cismont, Virginia.

Masthead of Virginia Gazette, Purdie & Dixon edition, February 22, 1770, page 1. The Colonial Williamsburg Foundation.

Detail of excerpt about burning of Jefferson's house, *Virginia Gazette*, Purdie & Dixon edition, February 22, 1770, page 3. The Colonial Williamsburg Foundation.

Mohogany Square English Pianoforte by Johannes Zumpe, London, 1766, accession #1968-294, image # DS93-412. The Colonial Williamsburg Foundation.

Marriage Bond of Thomas Jefferson, December 23, 1771. The Library of Virginia. Reproduction courtesy of The Colonial Williamsburg Foundation. (Scan from microfilm reel #M-1180.4)

Blenheim Claim House. Photographer Dan Friedman. Albemarle Monthly, March 1979, page 22.

Blenheim Claim House is now owned by Blenheim Vineyards, Charlottesville, Virginia.

Tobacco Boat (Batteau) from Tatham, William, *Historical and Practical Essay on the Culture and Commerce of Tobacco*, London, 1800. Image # 1990-619. Special Collections, John D. Rockefeller, Jr. Library, The Colonial Williamsburg Foundation.

Title page of *Summary View of Rights* of British America by Thomas Jefferson, Williamsburg: Printed by Clementina Rind, 1774. Image # D2012-COPY-0910-1007. Special Collections, John D. Rockefeller, Jr. Library, The Colonial Williamsburg Foundation.

The Ludwell-Paradise House. Image # D2009-BTL-0114-1045. The Colonial Williamsburg Foundation.

Masthead of *VIRGINIA GAZETTE,* Clementina Rind edition, April 21, 1774. Image #D2013-COPY-0102-1022. Special Collections, John D. Rockefeller, Jr. Library, The Colonial Williamsburg Foundation.

Map of Virginia Counties between 1761-1770. Atlas of County Boundary Changes in Virginia 1634-1895, by Michael F. Doran. Iberian Publishing Company 1987. The Albemarle-Charlottesville Historical Society

W202 Shadwell–Birthplace of Thomas Jefferson. Courtesy of the Virginia Department of Historic Resources, Richmond, Virginia.

Thomas Jefferson Birth Marker Shadwell. Author's personal photo library, courtesy of the Thomas Jefferson Foundation at Monticello.

View of Blenheim Vineyards, Charlottesville, Virginia. Courtesy of Jack Looney, Photographer.

Statue of Thomas Jefferson and Author Jayne D'Alessandro-Cox. Author's personal photo library, courtesy of the Colonial Williamsburg Foundation.

Text Sources

The Worlds of Thomas Jefferson at Monticello by Susan R. Stein. Harry N. Abrams, Inc. Publishers in association with the Thomas Jefferson Memorial Foundation, Inc., 1949.

The Eye of Thomas Jefferson by William Howard Adams, Editor. Thomas Jefferson Memorial Foundation, Inc., Charlottesville, Virginia and University of Missouri Press, Columbia and London, 1976.

The domestic life of Thomas Jefferson, by Sarah N. Randolph. The University of Virginia Press: Charlottesville, VA, 1978.

The Private Life of Thomas Jefferson, edited by Rev. Hamilton W. Pierson, DD, President of Cumberland College, Kentucky.

A Window on Williamsburg, text by John J. Walklet, Jr. and Thomas K. Ford. The Colonial Williamsburg Foundation, Williamsburg, Virginia, 1966.

The Architecture of Jefferson Country: Charlottesville and Albemarle County, Virginia, by K. Edward Lay. Charlottesville: University Press of Virginia, 2000.

Jefferson—A Monticello Sampler, by Rick Britton. Publisher: Mariner Companies, Inc., 2008.

Young Man from the Piedmont—the Youth of Thomas Jefferson, by Leonard Wibberly. Publisher: Ariel Books; 1st edition, 1963.

The World's True History, Vol. III, by Edgar Sanderson, American History, 1931.

In Pursuit of Reason, The Life of Thomas Jefferson, by Noble E. Cunningham, Jr.. Ballantine Books, 1987.

Surveyors and Statesmen, by Sarah Huhes. Publisher: Virginia Surveyors Foundation : Virginia Association of Surveyors, 1979.

Thomas Jefferson—The Apostle of Americanism, by Gilbert Chinard. Boston: Little, Brown And Company, 1929.

Thomas Jefferson–An Intimate History, by Fawn M. Brodie. New York: W.W. Norton and Company, 1974.

Jefferson the Virginian, Appendix I, by Dumas Malone. Boston: Little, Brown and Company, 1948

Peter Jefferson Will, *Albemarle County Will Book 2:32 The Papers of Thomas Jefferson, Jefferson's Memorandum Books.* Princeton: Princeton University Press, 1950, pg. 86-87.

A Genealogy of the Known Descendants of Robert Carter of Corotoman, by Florence Tyler Carlton. Publisher F.T. Carlton. 1982.

The Women Jefferson Loved, by Virginia Scharff. Harper Collins, 2010.

The Family Letters of Thomas Jefferson, edited by Edwin Morris Betts and James Adam Bear, Jr., Columbia: University of Missouri Press, 1966.

The Jefferson's at Shadwell, by Susan Kern, Ph.D. Yale University Press, 2010.

The Autobiographical Ana of Robley Dunglison, MD, by Samuel X. Radbill. Philadelphia: The American Philosophical Society, 1963.

Thomas Jefferson: A Life, by Willard Sterne Randall. Harper Collins Publishers, 1994.

Historic Roads of Virginia Albemarle County Roads 1725-1816, by Nathaniel Mason Pawlett. Virginia Highway & Transportation Research Council, 1981.

Some of Albemarle County's Roads circa 1745, by Nathaniel Mason Pawlett. 1978.

Atlas of County Boundary Changes in Virginia 1634-1895, by Michael F. Doran. Iberian Publishing Company 1987.

Geodaesia: or The Art of Surveying and Measuring of Land Made Easy, by John Love, London, 1688. Publisher: United States Historical Research Service, 1997.

Thomas Jefferson LAWYER, by Frank L. Dewey. University of Virginia Press, 1986.

Shirley Plantation, by the Shirley Plantation, Charles City, Virginia.

The Life and Works of Thomas Jefferson, Vol. II, No. 1, Part 3, by Leonard Liggio. George Mason University, 1999.

Passage Through the Garden, by John Logan Allen. Urbana: University of Illinois Press, 1975.

Exploring the West from Monticello, by Guy Meriwether Benson. Lincoln: University of Nebraska Press, 2003.

Lewis and Clark: The Maps of Exploration 1507-1814, by Guy Meriwether Benson, William R. Irving and Heather Moore Riser. Charlottesville: Howell Press, 2002.

Daniel Boone's predecessor in Kentucky, who was Dr. Thomas Walker of Albemarle County Virginia, by

Annie Walker Burns, Second edition, with additions. Washington, D.C., 1962.

History of the Five Indian Nations of Canada, by Cadwallader Colden. New York: Allerton Book Company, 1922.

Peter Jefferson, Gentleman, ca. 1949, by Edgar Charles Hickisch. Accession #825-a, Special Collections, University of Virginia Library, Charlottesville, VA.

The Fairfax Line: A Historic Landmark, by George W. Frye. Stephens City, VA: Commercial Press, 1990.

Colonel Joshua Fry of Virginia, by George W. Frye. Cincinnati, OH: n.p., 1966.

Map of the Inhabited Part of Virginia, containing the whole province of Maryland with Part of Pennsylvania, New Jersey and North Carolina, by Joshua Fry. Accession #A, 1751 .F79, Special Collections, University of Virginia Library, Charlottesville, VA.

Twelve Virginia Counties, by John Hastings Gwathmey. Richmond, VA: The Dietz Press, 1937.

Dr. Thomas Walker and the Loyal Company of Virginia, by Archibald Henderson. Worcester, MA: American Antiquarian Society, 1931.

Jefferson's Albemarle: A Guide to Albemarle County and the City of Charlottesville, Volumne 482. By Writers' Program (U.S.). Jarman's incorporated, printers. Charlottesville, VA: University of Virginia, 1941.

Old Churches and Families of Virginia: Volume 1, by Bishop Meade. Philadelphia: J.B. Lippincott Company, 1910.

Historic Homes of the South-West Mountains Virginia, by Edward C. Mead. Harrisonburg, VA: C.J. Carrier Company, 1978.

Albemarle: Jefferson's County, 1727-1976, by John Hammond Moore. Charlottesville, VA: University of Virginia Press, 1976.

The Albemarle of Other Days, by Mary Rawlings. Charlottesville: The Michie Company Publishers, 1925.

Memoir of Colonel Joshua Fry, by Philip Slaughter. Randolph and English: Richmond, VA, 1880.

The Rescue of the "Lady Slipper," by Gail Timberlake. Author House Publisher, 2010.

The Church Hymnal with Canticles (rare book), Edited by Rev. Charles L. Hutchins. Medford, Massachusettes. Published by the Editor, 1888. Love devine, all love excelling. page 456.

Hymns For Those That Seek and Those That Have Redemption In The Blood of Jesus Christ, by Charles Wesley, 1747. Hymn: Love Divine, All Loves Excelling.

Scottsville on the James, by Virginia Moore. Richmond: Dietz Press, 1994.

The Architecture of Jefferson County, by Edward K. Lay. University Press, Charlottesville, pages 9, 73.

Albemarle County Deed Book, No. 28, p. 24, 6, Nov. 1828, Charlottesville, Virginia.

Albemarle County Deed Book, No. 28, p. 286-287, Charlottesville, Virginia.

History of Albemarle, by Edgar Woods. p. 8-10, Bridgewater, VA: The Green Bookman, 1932.

Albemarle County Order Book, Virginia, 1745-1748, page 1, Charlottesville, Virginia.

Virginia House Tour, by William T. Stevens. Stevenpost Publication, Charlottesville, VA, 1962

Virginia Commission on Boundary Lines, 1728 & 1749, Accession #38-628, Special Collections, University of Virginia Library, Charlottesville, Virginia.

Journal of an Exploration in the Spring of the Year 1750, by Thomas Walker. Little, Brown, and Company. Boston, Mass., 1888. Accession# F 516 .W18 1888, Special Collections, University of Virginia Library, Charlottesville, Virginia.

Goochland County Deed Book 10:169-170, 12:217-219, Charlottesville, Virginia.

The Man Who Found Thoreau: Roland W. Robbins and the Rise of Historical Archaeology in America, by Donald W. Linebaugh. Durham, N.H.: University of New Hampshire Press, 2004.

People's Book of Biography, by James Parton, 1868. Submitted by Cathy Danielson.

Early American Turf Stock, 1730-1780. Richmond, Virginia: Old Dominion Press, 3 volumes, 1934.

Thomas Jefferson–A Revealing Biography, by Page Smith. Massachusetts Historical Society.

Thomas Jefferson's Memorandum Books: Accounts, with Legal Records & Miscellany, 1767-1826.

Jefferson's Farm Book. The Thomas Jefferson Foundation. See pp. 1-2. Charlottesville, Virginia.

Thomas Jefferson, Man on a Mountain, by Natalie S. Bober, 1993.

Thomas Jefferson's accounts with John Wayles, Fee Book, The Thomas Jefferson Foundation, Charlottesville, Virginia.

The History of Grace Church, Walker's Parish, by Barclay Rives. Charlottesville, Virginia: Papercraft, 1993.

A Picture Book of Thomas Jefferson, by David A. Adler. Holiday House Inc. Publisher: The Trumpet Club, 1991.

Young Thomas Jefferson by Francene Sabin and Robert Baxter, Sep 1997.

Mary Geddy's Day–A Colonial Girl in Williamsburg, by Kate Waters. Scholastic Press, NY, 1999.

Historic Communities Colonial Life, by Bobbie Kalman. Crabtree Publishing Company, 1992.

Thomas Jefferson–Third President of the United States, by Helen Albee Monsell. Aladdin Paperbacks, 1989.

Tom Jefferson–A Boy in Colonial Days, by Helen Albee Monsell. The Bobbs-Merrill Company Publishers. Dutton Children's Books. Division of Penguin Young Readers Group.

If You Lived in Williamsburg in Colonial Days, by Barbara Brennar. Scholastic Inc. and the Colonial Williamsburg Foundation, 2000.

Thomas Jefferson Treats Himself, by John M. Holmes. Loft Press, Inc, 1997.

Notable American Women, edited by Edward T James, Janet Wilson James, Paul S Boyer. The Belknap Press of Harvard University, Cambridge, Massachusetts. 1971.

Life in Old Virginia, by James Joseph McDonald. The Old Virginia Publishing Company, Norfolk, VA, 1907.

The Road to Monticello: The Life and Mind of Thomas Jefferson, by Kevin J. Hayes. New York: Oxford University Press, 2008.

The Life of Thomas Jefferson, by Henry S. Randall, 1858, Volume 1 (of the 3 Volumes).

The Papers of Thomas Jefferson, Second Series. Jefferson Memorandum Books, E332.8, .M46 1997 vol. 1 pages 3-380.

Life in Old Virginia, by James Joseph McDonald. The Old Virginia Publishing Company, Norfolk, VA, 1907.

The Autobiography of Thomas Jefferson, 1743-1790. Edited by Paul Leicester Ford. New Introduction by Michael Zuckerman, University of Pennsylvania Press.

Who Was Thomas Jefferson? by Dennis Brindell Fradin, Grosset & Dunlap, New York, 2003.

The Women Jefferson Loved, by Virginia Scharff. Harper Collins Publishers, 2011.

Some Colonial Mansions and Those Who Lived in Them, by Thomas Allen Glenn. Philadelphia: H.T. Coates & Company, 1900.

Defiant Peacemaker: Nicholas Trist in the Mexican War, by Wallace Ohrt. College Station: Texas A&M University Press, 1997.

The Quotable Jefferson, Collected and Edited by John P. Kaminski. Pages 176-181, 2006.

Thomas Jefferson encyclopedia Life Portraits Book. Artist, John Trumbull's original Declaration of Independence showing Jefferson painted from life, winter of 1787-88 at Jefferson's Paris residence. The Yale University Art Gallery.

Thomas Jefferson Memorial Foundation Archives, Series 11: Jefferson Birthplace Memorial Park Commission ("Shadwell"). Jefferson Library, Charlottesville, Virginia.

In Defense of Thomas Jefferson: The Sally Hemings Sex Scandal, by William G. Hyland, Jr., Thomas Dunne Books, St. Martin's Press, New York, 2009.

The Thomas Jefferson Papers at the Library of Congress–Topic: The American Revolution.

Thomas Jefferson: Statesman of Science, by Silvio Bedini, p. 53. New York: MacMillan Publishing Co., 1990.

Recipes from the Raleigh Tavern Bakery, by The Colonial Williamsburg Foundation. Williamsburg, Virginia, 1984.

Natural Bridge and Natural Bridge Caverns–Guidebook, by Edgar W. Spencer, Professor Emeritus of Geology, William and Lee University, Poor House Mountain Press, 2011.

The Works of Thomas Jefferson, Federal Edition. New York and London, G.P. Putnam's Sons, 1904-5. Volume 1.

Jefferson, by Saul K. Padover. Harcourt, Brace and Company, New York, 1942.

Articles Sources

Papers of R. E. Lee and Son, Albert and Shirley Small Special Collections Library, University of Virginia.

Magazine of Albemarle County History, v.21, 1962-63. Article entitled—The Albemarle County Court House by lawyer, historian and past President of the Albemarle County Historical Society, Bernard P. Chamberlain.

Magazine of Albemarle County History, article entitled-Albemarle County in Virginia by Edgar Woods, Charlottesville, 1901; pp. 27,60.

Magazine of Albemarle County History, article entitled-The Albemarle of Other Days by Mary Rawlings, Charlottesville, 1925; pp. 30-32, pp. 34-35.

Magazine of Albemarle County History, article entitled–Early Charlottesville: Recollections of James Alexander, 1828-1874, Charlottesville, 1942; pg. 1.

"Last Few Days in the Life of Thomas Jefferson," by James A. Bear, Jr., *Magazine of Albemarle County History*, 32 (1974): 63-79.

"Thomas Mann Randolph, Piedmont Plowman," William H. Gaines, Jr., Papers of the Albemarle County Historical Society, 11:39

"Where Did the Indians Sleep?: An Archaeological & Ethno-historical Study of Mid-Eighteenth Century Piedmont Virginia," by Susan Kern, Ph. D..

"Thomas Jefferson: A Personal Financial Biography," by Steven Harold Hochman, PhD diss., University of Virginia, 1987.

"The Material World of the Jeffersons at Shadwell," by Susan Kern, Ph.D.

"Will of John Wayles." *Tyler's Quarterly Magazine* 6(3):268-270.

"Thomas Jefferson, Son of Virginia," article by Dennis Montgomery. *The Colonial Williamsburg Journal, 1993.*

"Letters of Francis Jerdone," *William and Mary Quarterly*, 1st ser., 16, no. 2 (October 1907): 127-28.

"Dabney Carr: Portrait of a Colonial Patriot, by Williams S. Simpson, Jr., " Virginia Cavalcade 23 (Winter 1974): 5-13, 1974.

"The Two Viewmonts," by Frederick D. Nichols. Papers of the Albemarle County Historical Society, Charlottesville, Virginia. Volume XI, 1950-1951, and Volume XIII, 1953, pg. 23.

"In Search of Jefferson's Birthplace," by Fiske Kimball, *Virginia Magazine of History and Biography* 51, No. 4 (1943): 313-325.

"The Wayles Family," by Jefferson Malone, 1:432-433, Appendix 1D.

"John Wayles Rates His Neighbors," by John M. Hemphill, II, ed., *VMHB* 66(3):302-306.

"Shadwell' Represents 20 Years of Investigation," by Jean Bruns. Charlottesville, Virginia. *Daily Progress*, June 30, 1961.

"Pick-and-Shovel Historian," by Evan Jones. *Collier's*, August 5, 1955.

"A New Jefferson Shrine in Virginia," by John E. Long. *New York Times*, January 7, 1962.

"Shadwell–Jefferson's Birthplace." *Iron Worker* (Autumn 1962): 1-7.

Papers of the Thomas Jefferson Chapter of the Virginia Society of the Sons of the American Revolution, 1987-1998, Accession #343-r, Special Collections Dept., University of Virginia Library, Charlottesville, Virginia.

Papers of Walker, his son, Francis Walker, and the Walker and Page families, 1742-1886, Accession #3098, Special Collections, University of Virginia Library, University of Virginia, Charlottesville, Virginia.

Charlottesville Observer, April 15, 1993, Albemarle Living Section, page 12.

John Wayles Will and Codicil, Charles City County Deeds and Wills, 1766-1774, pp. 461-462.

Thomas Walker of Albemarle, by Natalie J. Disbrow. Papers of the Albemarle County Historical Society. Volume 1, Charlottesville, Virginia, 1941.

Thomas Walker Papers, 1744-1835, Accession #9996, University of Virginia Library, Charlottesville, Virginia.

Abstracts of Title to Shadwell Properties, 1735-1945, Accession #5087, University of Virginia Library, Charlottesville, Virginia.

Monticello Research Report, by Russell L. Martin, June 7, 1988.

Jefferson's Albemarle: History of Albemarle County, VA, 1727-1819. Ph.D. diss., by William Minor Dabney, University of Virginia, 1951.

Franklin and Fesler, Historical Archaelogy, 31-46.

Article regarding Natural Bridge is courtesy of Thomas Jefferson Encyclopedia, written by Lucia Stanton, Monticello Research Report, April 1995.

Article regarding Natural Bridge purchase is courtesy of Thomas Jefferson Encyclopedia, based on RLB, Research Report, March 1997.

Recipes from the Raleigh Tavern Bakery by The Colonial Williamsburg Foundation, Williamsburg, Virginia. © 1984

Web Sites Sources

Tate Publishing & Enterprises, www.tatepublishing.com

The Colonial Williamsburg Foundation, www.colonial williamsburg.com

The Earl Gregg Swem Library, The College of William & Mary, www.swem.wm.edu

The Thomas Jefferson Foundation, www.monticello.org

Tuckahoe Plantation, www.tuckahoeplantation.com

Blenheim Vineyards, blenheimvineyards.com/

Blenheim Vineyards history, www.blenheimvineyards. com/images/PrivateEvents/Blenheim-Hou...

Rosewell, www.rosewell.org

The Monticello Vegetable Garden, www.monticello. org/site/house-and-gardens/vegetable-garden

Natural Bridge – Thomas Jefferson's Monticello, www. monticello.org

Natural Bridge, Virginia, www.naturalbridgeva.com/ The_Natural_Bridge_Fact_Sheet_6_11.pdf

Gold and Silver Standards, www.cyberussr.com/hcunn/ gold-std.html

Thomas Jefferson's *Notes on the State of Virginia*: ch.V, xroads.virginia.edu/~hyper/jefferson/ch05.html

Grace Episcopal Church, www.gracekeswick.org

Shirley Plantation, www.shirleyplantation.com

Shirley Plantation, www.research.history.org/JDRLibrary /SpecialCollections/SpecialCollectionsDocs/ ShirleyPP.cfm

The Albemarle Charlottesville Historical Society, www. albemarlehistory.org

Smithsonian Institution, www.si.edu

The Scottsville Museum, www.smuseum.avenue.org

Virginia Department of Historic Resources, www.dhr. virginia.gov

Colonial Williamsburg, www.history.org/

Colonial Williamsburg, en.wikipedia.org/wiki/Colonial Williamsburg

Colonial Williamsburg, www.colonialwilliamsburg.com/

Colonial Williamsburg, www.history.org/history/index. cfm

Free Workmen, www.monticello.org › Plantation & Slavery › People of the Plantation

Albemarle County, archive.org/stream/cu319240287 85703/cu31924028785703dj…

William Randolph, www.ritger.com/genealogy/getperson. php?personID=I20435&…

Descendants of Thomas Jefferson, www.homepages. rootsweb.ancestry.com/—madcuzns/jefftree.htm

The Curles Area of Virginia, www.geni.com/projects/ Colonizing-Virginia-Curles-of-the…

Peter Jefferson ancestry, www.monticello.org/site/ research-and-collections/jeffer…

Peter Jefferson biography, www.monticello.org/site/jefferson/peter-jefferson

Peter Jefferson ancestry, www.lva.virginia.gov/exhibits/fry-jefferson/peterJeffer...

Peter Jefferson, www.surveyhistory.org/peterjefferson1.htm

Peter Jefferson ancestry, www2.vcdh.virginia.edu/lewisandclark/students/projects/...

The Loyal Land Company, www.virginiaplaces.org/settleland/landloyal.html

The Ohio Company, www.ohiohistorycentral.org/entry.php?rec=944

The Mississippi Land Company, www.mountvernon.org/educational-resources/encyclopedia/...

Middling Planter, research.history.org/HistoricalResearch/ResearchTheme...

Surveyor Measuring Chains, www.surveyhistory.org/changingchains.htm

Planting Tobacco, www.nps.gov/jame/historyculture/tobacco-colonial-cultiv...

Factor Store, www.baygateways.net/general.cfm?id=5

History of Shadwell, www.charlottesville-area-real-estate.com/ShadwellVirgi...

Shadwell, www.monticello.org/site/research-and-collections/shadwe...

Clifton, www.cliftonInn.net

John Rolphe, www.apva.org/history/jrolfe.html

Tobacco Inspection Stations, www.charlescity.org/historical-markers-state2.shtml

Tobacco Terminology, www.history.org/history/teaching/enewsletter/volume2/im...

William Randolph and Maria Judith Page Genealogy www.bellsouthpwp.net/b/p/bprest/wrand.htm

Lewis and Clark, www.lib.virginia.edu/speccol/exhibits/lewisclark/exploring/ch3-16.html

Lewis and Clark, www2.lib.virginia.edu/exhibits/lewisclark/exploring/ch...

Lewis and Clark, www.lib.virginia.edu/speccol/exhibits/lewisclark/albemarle2.html

Lewis and Clark, www2.vcdh.virginia.edu/lewisandclark/students/projects/adventurers/maurybio.html

Lewis and Clark, www.monticello.org/site/jefferson/lewis-and-clark-exped...

Cherokee Indian Chief Ostenaco, www.en.wikipedia.org/wiki/Ostenaco

Cherokee Indian Chief Ostenaco, www.tn4me.org/sapage.cfm/said/75/eraid/2/majorid/7/.../62

Cherokee Indian Chief Ostenaco, www.epinions.com/content545630883460

Lte. Henry Timberlake, www.epinions.com/content545630883460

College of William & Mary, www.wm.edu/about/jefferson/jeffersoncollege.php -

Early years 1743-1766, www.sparknotes.com/biography/jefferson/timeline.html

The Educational Work of Thomas Jefferson, www.archive.org/stream/educationalworko012284mbp/educationalworko012284mbpdjvu.txt

Three Notch'd Road, www.henricohistoricalsociety.org/threechopt.html

Three Notch'd Road, www.waldo.jaquith.org/blog/2009/02/three-chopt-road/

The Tuckahoe Plant, www.werelate.org/wiki/Analysis: TuckahoePlaceNameFreq...

Tuckahoe, www.nps.gov/nr/travel/jamesriver/tuk.htm

Tuckahoe, www.monticello.org/site/research-and-collections/tuckah...

Tuckahoe, www.historictuckahoe.com/ourhistory.html

Tuckahoe Dendrochronology, www.nps.gov/nr/travel/jamesriver/text.htm

Isaac Granger Jefferson, www.monticello.org › ... › Enslaved People › Workers

Isaac Granger Jefferson, www.monticello.org/getting-word/people/isaac-granger-jefferson?...

Thomas Mann Randolph and Ann Cary, www.freepages.genealogy.rootsweb.ancestry.com/—mysouthernfa...

Joshua Fry, www2.vcdh.virginia.edu/lewisandclark/students/projects/.../frybio.ht...

Joshua Fry/Viewmont, www.newrivernotes.com/va/aod.htm

Thomas Jefferson Quotes, www.marksquotes.com/Founding-Fathers/Jefferson/

Thomas Walker Explorer, www.ask.com/wiki/Thomas Walker

Isaac Granger Jefferson, www.monticello.org/site/plantation-and-slavery/isaac-gr...

Dabney Carr, www.wiki.monticello.org/mediawiki/index.php/DabneyCarr(17...

Snowden, www.monticello.org/site/research-and-collections/snowden

Elizabeth Jefferson, www.monticello.org/site/jefferson/elizabeth-jefferson

Captain Isham Randolph Ancestry, www.wc.rootsweb.ancestry.com/cgi-bin/igm.cgi?op=GET&db=monk...

Scottsville Bridge, www.scottsvillemuseum.com/transportation/homeRollOneNeg23A....

Scottsville Bridge, www.smuseum.avenue.org/ourhistory/home.html

Scott's Landing, www.smuseum.avenue.org/about/home.html

Scott's Landing, www.grandlodgeofvirginia.org/lodges/45/history.asp

Snowden and Scottsville, Virginia, www.scottsvillemuseum.com/homes/homeRollTenNeg16A.html

Charlottesville and Scottsville, Virginia, www.visitcharlottesville.org/listings/index.cfm?action=...

Randolph Jefferson, www.monticello.org/site/jefferson/randolph-jefferson

Tobacco Transportation in Colonial Times, www.munseys.com/diskseven/toba.pdf

Batteau, www.secondalbany.org/2ndalbanymainalbanybateau.html

Batteau, www.vacanals.org/batteau/batteauconstruction/tobaccotrans...

Batteau, www.ask.com/wiki/Bateau

Shipping Transportation, www.virginiaplaces.org/transportation/colonialshipping....

Early Virginia River Trade, www.earlyamerica.com/review/winter2000/trade.html

Scottsville Museum, www.scottsvillemuseum.com/homes/homeRollTenNeg16A.html

Martha Wayles-Skelton, www.monticello.org/site/jefferson/martha-wayles-skelton...

Marriage Bond, www.oocities.org/heartland/hills/5425/tj-marriage-bond.html

Wedding Bonds, www.pipeline.com/—richardpence/bonds2.htm

Shadwell, www.monticello.org/site/research-and-collections/shadwe...

Martha Jefferson, www.genealogytrails.com/main/presidents/biosmarthajefferson

Jefferson's Riding horses, www.monticello.org/site/research-and-collections/horses

Elizabeth Jefferson, www.monticello.org/site/jefferson/elizabeth-jefferson

James Maury Biography, www2.vcdh.virginia.edu/lewisandclark/students/projects/...

Lewis and Clark, www2.lib.virginia.edu/exhibits/lewisclark/exploring/ch...

John Wayles, www.monticello.org/site/jefferson/john-wayles

John Wayles, www.ask.com/wiki/JohnWayles

John Wayles' wives, b-womeninamericanhistory18.blogspot.com/2011/09/thomas-...

Martha Wayles Skelton, www.monticello.org/site/jefferson/martha-wayles-skelton

Martha Skelton Jefferson – The Jefferson Legacy Foundation, www.jeffersonlegacy.org/commentary.html

Bermuda Hundred, www.petersburghistory.org/index.php?option=comcontent&...

Hymnal, www.cyberhymnal.org/htm/l/d/ldalexcl.htm

Earthquakes, www.dmme.virginia.gov/DMR3/major-vaearthquakes.shtml

Jane Randolph Jefferson, www.monticello.org/site/jefferson/jane-randolph-jeffers...

Randolph Geneology, www.homepages.rootsweb.ancestry.com/—marshall/esmd18.htm

Rosewell, www.rosewell.org/timeline.shtml

Bursar Book entry for Thomas Jefferson, The College of William & Mary, http://hdl.handle.net/10288/13360

www.thefamouspeople.com/profiles/thomas-jefferson-72.ph...

The Jefferson Legacy Foundation, www.jeffersonlegacy.org/commentary.html

First Ladies, www.firstladies.org/biographies/firstladies.aspx?biogra...

Quotes by Thomas Jefferson, www.brainyquote.com/quotes/authors/t/thomasjefferson.h...

Thomas Jefferson – Autobiography, hypermall.com/LibertyOnline/Jefferson/Autobiography.htm...

Thomas Jefferson, www.math.virginia.edu/Jefferson/jeffr.htm

Thomas Jefferson, sc94.ameslab.gov/TOUR/tjefferson.html

Thomas Jefferson, www.monticello.org/site/research-and-collections/jeffer...

Thomas Jefferson, www.monticello.org/site/research-and-collections/john-h...

Dictionary definition of British currency abbreviations, www.dictionary.reference.com/browse/l.s.d.

Hurricanes, www.hurricaneville.com/historic.html

The Free Information Society, www.freeinfosociety.
com/site.php?postnum=636

Thomas Jefferson's Wife Martha, www.b-women-
inamericanhistory18.blogspot.com/2011/09/
thomas-...

Poplar Forest, www.poplarforestllc.com/

Poplar Forest, www.poplarforest.org/sites/default/files/
PFArchaeologyI...

City of Charlottesville-Three Notch'd Road, www.
charlottesville.org/Index.aspx?page=1978

City of Charlottesville-Three Notch'd Road, www.dhr.
virginia.gov/hiwaymarkers/hwmarkerinfo.htm

The Route of Three Notch'd Road, www.virginiadot.
org/defaultnoflash.asp

Rivanna River, www.rivannariver.org

Wetherburn's Tavern at Williamsburg, www.history.
org/almanack/places/hb/hbweth.cfm

Fry-Jefferson Map, www.encyclopediavirginia.org/
Fry-JeffersonMapofVirgi...

Fry-Jefferson Map, www.lva.virginia.gov/exhibits/
fry-jefferson/fry-jeffers...

Autobiography of Thomas Jefferson, libertyonline.
hypermall.com/Jefferson/Autobiography.html

Inoculation, www.monticello.org/site/research-and-
collections/inocul...

Thomas Jefferson Encyclopedia, www.wiki.monticello.
org/mediawiki/index.php/FamilyHistory

Plantation and Slavery, www.monticello.org/site/plan-
tation-and-slavery/jupiter-... \

City of Charlottesville Awards and Recognitions, www.
charlottesville.org/Index.aspx?page=158

Urban History of Charlottesville, www2.iath.virginia.edu/schwartz/cville/cville.history.h...

Thomas Jefferson Timeline of Important Dates, www.shmoop.com/thomas-jefferson/timeline.html

Raleigh Tavern, www.history.org/almanack/places/hb/hbral.cfm

Raleigh Tavern, www.history.org/foundation/journal/jeffart.cfm

The Stamp Act of 1765, www.constitution.org/bcp/virres1765.htm

Resolutions of 1765, www.ushistory.org/declaration/related/henry.htm

Resolutions of 1765, www.ask.com/wiki/VirginiaResolves

Fluvanna River, www.sevenislandshistory.com/

Thomas Jefferson Birthplace, www.monticello.org/site/about/jefferson-birthplace-memo...

Thomas Jefferson Memorial Foundation Archives, Series 11: Jefferson Birthplace Memorial Park Commission ("Shadwell"). Jefferson Library, Charlottesville, Va., www.monticello.org/site/about/jefferson-birthplace-memo...

Thomas Jefferson's Riding Horse, www.archive.org/stream/memoirsofamontic031158mbp/memoirsofa...

Henry de Bracton, www.ask.com/wiki/HenrydeBracton

Sir Edward Coke, www.britannica.com/EBchecked/topic/124844/Sir-Edward-Co...

Printer and Binder Colonial Williamsburg, www.history.org/almanack/life/trades/tradepri.cfm

Small Pox Vaccine, www.Wilipedia.

Randolph-Jefferson, www.monticello.org/site/jefferson/randolph-jefferson

Wren Building, www.wm.edu/about/history/historic campus/wrenbuilding/in...

Oratory Skills, www.blog.coherentia.com/index. php/2010/01/reviving-the-anci...

Moot Court, www.lawschool.about.com/od/lawschool culture/a/mootcourt.htm

Alexander Pope's Poem The Rape of the Lock, www.librivox.org/the-rape-of-the-lock-by-alexander-pope/

Parishes of Virginia, www.vagenweb.org/parishes.htm

Plant Quotation by Thomas Jefferson, www.monticello. org/site/jefferson/useful-plant-quotatio...

Joshua Fry, www.encyclopediavirginia.org/FryJoshuaca 1700-May31...

George Wythe, www.hobnobblog.com/2012/05/12/ george-wythe-teacher-of-liber...

A New Abridgment of the Law, www.rookebooks. com/product?prodid=4575

Price of Tobacco, www.redhill.org/biography.html

Thomas Jefferson's Library of Books 1771, www. tjlibraries.monticello.org/transcripts/skipwith/ skipwit...

Old English Money, www.obsoleteskills.wikispot.org/ Makingchangeinshillingsandpence

St. Anne's Parish, www.archive.org/stream/oldchurches minis003253mbp/oldchurche...

Henrico County, www.wimfamhistory.net/Virginia/ virgin02.htm

Belmont mansion, www.archive.org/stream/historichomes o00mead/historichom...

Wayland's Crossing, www.hallowedground.org/Explore-the-Journey/Historic-Tow...

Transatlantic Sailing, www.virginiaplaces.org/transportation/colonialshipping....

Fluvanna River, www.sevenislandshistory.com/

Cucullin, www.monticello.org/site/blog-and-community/posts/welshn...

Flat Hat Club, www.monticello.org/site/research-and-collections/frater...

Rhetoric, www.speaklikeapro.co.uk/Rhetoric&Public Speakin...

Last letter to James Madison, www.blog.pacificlegal.org/2012/happy-birthday-sir-edward-co...

Tyranny of Slave Children, www.revolutionary-war-and-beyond.com/thomas-jefferson-q...

Summary View of the Rights of British America, www.history.org/almanack/people/bios/biojeff1.cfm

Ambler wedding date, www.dcodriscoll.pbworks.com/w/page/24903483/Ambler

Natural Bridge, www.lewis-clark.org/content/content-article.asp?ArticleID=1752

Natural Bridge, www.coursesite.uhcl.edu/hsh/whitec/litr/5535/sylsched/tjnatbridge.htm

Natural Bridge, www.en.wikipedia.org/wiki/Natural Bridge(Virginia)

Natural Bridge, www.monticello.org/site/research-and-collections/natura...

Mrs. Drummond, www.jeffersonlegacy.org/commentary.html

Quarter Farms, www.monticello.org/site/plantation-and-slavery/quarter-...

Monticello construction, www.monticello.org/site/house-and-gardens/monticello-ho...

Robert Carter's daughter...Judith Carter Page, www.christchurch1735.org/history/robertcarter.html

Robert "King" Carter, www.geni.com/people/Col-Robert-King-Carter/600000000102...

Robert "King" Carter, nominihallslavelegacy.com/history-of-the-carter-family/...

Thomas Jefferson Quotes, www.monticello.org/site/research-and-collections/tje/quotations

Thomas Jefferson's Library, myloc.gov/exhibitions/jeffersonslibrary/

Ludwell-Paradise House, www.history.org/almanack/places/hb/hbludw.cfm

Clementina Rind, Printer, www.vahistorical.org/publications/historycornerrind.ht...

Public Domain for Free Music, www.pdinfo.com/PD-Music-Genres/PD-Hymn-Search.php

Lyrics for Love Divine, All Love Excelling, www.hymnsite.com/lyrics/umh384.sht

Virginia Highway Markers, www.dhr.virginia.gov/hiwaymarkers/hwmarkerinfo.htm

Shadwell Highway Marker W-202, www.dhr.virginia.gov/hiwaymarkers/marker.cfm?mid=4245

Thomas Jefferson's personal copy of the Summary View of the Rights of British America, www.wdl.org/en/item/117/

Contents of the Summary View of the Rights of British America, www.libertyonline.hypermall.com/Jefferson/Summaryview.

Intolerable Acts, www.militaryhistory.about.com/od/worldwar1/p/jutland.htl

Peter Jefferson biography, www.monticello.org/site/jefferson/peter-jefferson

Jane Randolph Jefferson biography, www.monticello.org/site/jefferson/jane-randolph-jeffers...

Date Jane Randolph Jefferson's birth according to Bible, www.womenhistoryblog.com/2008/11/jane-randolph-jefferso...

Daugther Jane Jefferson's Death, www.pbs.org/jefferson/archives/interviews/frame.htm

Mary Jefferson Bollings Biography, www.monticello.org/site/jefferson/mary-jefferson-bollin...

Thomas Jefferson death information, wiki.answers.com/Q/HowdidThomasJeffersondie

Elizabeth Jefferson Biography, www.monticello.org/site/jefferson/elizabeth-jefferson

Martha Jefferson Carr Burial Information, www.findagrave.com/cgi-bin/fg.cgi?page=gr&GRid=6883934

Martha Jefferson Carr and Children..., www.monticello.org/site/jefferson/our-breakfast-table

Lucy Jefferson Lewis gravesite, www.findagrave.com/cgi-bin/fg.cgi?page=gr&GRid=17409353

Anna Scott Jefferson Marks biography, www.monticello.org/site/jefferson/anne-scott-jefferson-...

Randolph Jefferson biography, www.monticello.org/site/jefferson/randolph-jefferson

Thomas Jefferson's Canons of Conduct, www.monticello.org › Jefferson › Quotations › Famous Quotations

Endnotes

1 Letter from Thomas Jefferson to Thomas Jefferson Smith, Monticello, February 21, 1825. *The Writings of Thomas Jefferson*, edited by H.A. Washington, Cabridge University Press, September 2011.

2 *Thomas Jefferson's Farm Book* and the *Jefferson Memorandum Books: Accounts, with Legal Records and Miscellany,1767–1826.*

3 *The Autobiography of Thomas Jefferson*, written January 6, 1821.

4 Ibid.

5 Letter from Thomas Jefferson to John Adams, October 14, 1816.

6 *The domestic life of Thomas Jefferson*, by great-granddaughter Sarah N. Randolph. (Compiled from family letters and reminiscences.) Charlottesville: University Press of Virginia, pub in 1871, reprint in 1978.

7 From the *Memorandum Book* of Nicholas Trist, close friend of Thomas Jefferson. *Defiant Peacemaker: Nicholas Trist in the Mexican War,*

by Wallace Ohrt, College Station: Texas A&M University Press, 1997.

8   *The Autobiography of Thomas Jefferson*, written January 6, 1821.

9   Thomas Jefferson's *Notes on the State of Virginia*, Query 18, 1871.

10 *The Autobiography of Thomas Jefferson*, written January 6, 1821.

11 *The domestic life of Thomas Jefferson*, by great-granddaughter Sarah N. Randolph, page 23. Charlottesville: University Press of Virginia, pub in 1871, reprint in 1978.

12 *The Autobiography of Thomas Jefferson*, written January 6, 1821.

13 Letter to Thomas Jefferson Randolph, 1808. *The Writings of Thomas Jefferson,* edited by H.A. Washington, Cabridge University Press, September 2011.

14 *The Autobiography of Thomas Jefferson*, written January 6, 1821.

15 *The Writings of Thomas Jefferson*, edited by H.A. Washington, Cabridge University Press, September 2011.

16 Letter to executor John Harvie, written January 14, 1760. *The Writings of Thomas Jefferson,* edited by H.A. Washington, Cabridge University Press, September 2011.

17 Letter to Thomas McAuley, dated June 14, 1819. Thomas Jefferson confirms his membership in the Flat Hat Club. *The Writings of Thomas Jefferson,* edited by H.A. Washington, Cabridge University Press, September 2011.

18 Letter to Dr. William Small, May 7, 1775, *The Writings of Thomas Jefferson,* edited by H.A. Washington, Cabridge University Press, September 2011.

19 Letter from Thomas Jefferson written to Thomas Mann Randolph, Jr., 1786. *The Writings of Thomas Jefferson,* edited by H.A. Washington, Cabridge University Press, September 2011.

20 Letter from Thomas Jefferson written to Peter Carr, August 19, 1785. *The Writings of Thomas Jefferson,* edited by H.A. Washington, Cabridge University Press, September 2011.

21 Letter from Thomas Jefferson written to Robert Skipwith, from Monticello, August 3, 1771. *The Writings of Thomas Jefferson*, edited by H.A. Washington, Cabridge University Press, September 2011.

22 *The Autobiography of Thomas Jefferson*, written January 6, 1821.

23 Letter from Thomas Jefferson written to L.H. Girardin from Monticello, January 15, 1815. *The Writings of Thomas Jefferson,* edited by H.A. Washington, Cabridge University Press, September 2011.

24 Ibid.

25 Ibid.

26 Ibid.

27 Letter from Thomas Jefferson to John Page, 1763. The Writings of Thomas Jefferson, edited by H.A. Washington, Cabridge University Press, September 2011.

28 Letter from Thomas Jefferson from Monticello to James Madison, February 17, 1826. *The Writings of Thomas Jefferson*, edited by H.A. Washington, Cabridge University Press, September 2011.

29 *The Autobiography of Thomas Jefferson*, written January 6, 1821.

30 Letter from Thomas Jefferson from Shadwell to John Page, December 25, 1762. *The Writings of Thomas Jefferson*, edited by H.A. Washington, Cabridge University Press, September 2011.

31 Letter from Thomas Jefferson from Shadwell to John Page, January 20, 1763. *The Writings of Thomas Jefferson*, edited by H.A. Washington, Cabridge University Press, September 2011.

32 Ibid.

33 Letter from Thomas Jefferson to John Page, January 20, 1763, with postscripts added February 12 and March 11, before mailing. *The Writings of Thomas Jefferson*, edited by H.A. Washington, Cabridge University Press, September 2011.

34 Letter from Thomas Jefferson from Shadwell to John Page, July 15, 1763. *The Writings of Thomas Jefferson,* edited by H.A. Washington, Cabridge University Press, September 2011.

35 Letter from Thomas Jefferson from Shadwell to John Page, July 15, 1763. *The Writings of Thomas Jefferson,* edited by H.A. Washington, Cabridge University Press, September 2011.

36 *Letter from Thomas Jefferson to John Page, October 7, 1763. The Writings of Thomas Jefferson,* edited by H.A. Washington, Cabridge University Press, September 2011.

37 Letter from Thomas Jefferson to John Page, January 19, 1764. *The Writings of Thomas Jefferson,* edited by H.A. Washington, Cabridge University Press, September 2011.

38 Letter from Thomas Jefferson to John Page, January 23, 1764. *The Writings of Thomas Jefferson,* edited by H.A. Washington, Cabridge University Press, September 2011.

39 Letter from Thomas Jefferson to William Fleming, March 20, 1764. *The Writings of Thomas Jefferson,* edited by H.A. Washington, Cabridge University Press, September 2011.

40 *Memoir, Correspondence And Miscellanies: From The Papers Of Thomas Jefferson*, by grandson, Thomas Jefferson Randolph, 1829. It was the first collection of Jefferson's writings.

41 *The Autobiography of Thomas Jefferson*, written January 21, 1821.

42 Ibid.

43 Letter from Thomas Jefferson to William Wirt, August 5, 1805. *The Writings of Thomas Jefferson*, edited by H.A. Washington, Cabridge University Press, September 2011.

44 Inscription written on Jane Jefferson's tomb, dedicated to her by Thomas Jefferson, originally written by poet William Shenstone.

45 Letter from Thomas Jefferson to Thomas Cooper, November 2, 1822. *The Writings of Thomas Jefferson*, edited by H.A. Washington, Cabridge University Press, September 2011.

46 *Jefferson's Memorandum Books: Accounts, with Legal Records and Miscellany.* 1767; and Thomas Jefferson's *Notes on the State of Virginia*, page 24.

47 Ibid.

48 *The Autobiography of Thomas Jefferson*, written January 6, 1821.

49 Ibid.

50 Letter from Thomas Jefferson to M. Silvestre, secretary of the Agricultural Society of Paris, Washington, May 29, 1807. The original quote is, "Attached to agriculture by inclination as well as by a conviction that it is the most useful of the occupations of man, my course of life has

not permitted me to add to its theories the lessons of practice."

51 Thomas Jefferson Memorandum of Services to My Country, after 2 September 1800.

52 Letter from Thomas Jefferson to Martha Jefferson Randolph, July 7, 1793. *The Writings of Thomas Jefferson,* edited by H.A. Washington, Cabridge University Press, September 2011.

53 Letter written to James Ogilvie, February 20, 1771, The Papers of Thomas Jefferson, 1:63.

54 Letter from Thomas Jefferson written to John Page, February 21, 1770. *The Writings of Thomas Jefferson,* edited by H.A. Washington, Cabridge University Press, September 2011.

55 Ibid.

56 Ibid.

57 From the collection of The Adams-Jefferson Letters. Original quote, "I cannot live without books: but fewer will suffice where amusement, and not use, is the only future object."

58 Letter from Thomas Jefferson from Monticello to Robert Skipwith on August 3, 1771. Thomas Jefferson's Suggested Book list. *The Writings of Thomas Jefferson,* edited by H.A. Washington, Cabridge University Press, September 2011.

59 Letter from Thomas Jefferson to Thomas Adams, May 1771. From the collection of *The Adams–Jefferson Letters: The Complete Correspondence*

Between Thomas Jefferson and Abigail and John Adams, edited by Lester J. Cappon.

60 Letter from Thomas Jefferson from Monticello to Robert Skipp, August 3, 1771. *The Writings of Thomas Jefferson*, edited by H.A. Washington, Cabridge University Press, September 2011.

61 Marriage License written by Thomas Jefferson, December 23, 1771.

62 *The Autobiography of Thomas Jefferson*, written January 6, 1821.

63 *The domestic life of Thomas Jefferson*, by Sarah N. Randolph. Charlottesville: University Press of Virginia, pub in 1871, reprint in 1978.

64 *Jefferson Fee Book, 1764–1790*.

65 Ibid.

66 Ibid.

67 Letter from Thomas Jefferson to friend John Page, Feb. 21, 1770. *The Papers of Thomas Jefferson*, Author: P. Boyd Publisher: Princeton University Press, New Jersey.

68 Inscription on Dabney Carr's grave marker at Monticello graveyard, May 28, 1773.

69 Inscription of bronze plate that Thomas Jefferson had made to nail on Thomas and Dabney's favorite tree, May 28, 1773.

70 *Life of Thomas Jefferson, Volume 1*, by Henry Stephens Randall. New York: Derby & Jackson, 1858.

71 *The Papers of Thomas Jefferson, Volume II*, (1955). Author: P. Boyd Publisher: Princeton University Press New Jersey.

72 *The Autobiography of Thomas Jefferson*, Notes on Virginia, p. 7, written January 6, 1821.

73 *Jefferson's Memorandum Books: Accounts, with Legal Records and Miscellany,1767-1826.*

74 Ibid.

75 *Jefferson's Memorandum Books: Accounts, with Legal Records and Miscellany, 1767-1826.*

76 Ibid.

77 Ibid.

78 *Jefferson's Memorandum Books: Accounts, with Legal Records and Miscellany.* March 10, 1774.

79 Thomas Jefferson's Canons of Conduct, written in letter to granddaughter Cornelia Jefferson Randolph, approximately 1811. *The Writings of Thomas Jefferson*, edited by H.A. Washington, Cabridge University Press, September 2011.

80 Jefferson's Memorandum Books: Jefferson's Account Book, April 29, 1775.

81 *The Autobiography of Thomas Jefferson*, written January 6, 1821.

82 Letter from Thomas Jefferson to cousin John Garland Jefferson, June 11, 1790. *The Writings of Thomas Jefferson*, edited by H.A. Washington, Cabridge University Press, September 2011.

83 Letter from Thomas Jefferson from Paris to Thomas Mann Randolph, Jr., August 27, 1786. *The Writings of Thomas Jefferson,* edited by H.A. Washington, Cabridge University Press, September 2011.

84 *Plan of Philip Mazzei's Agricultural Company by Thomas Jefferson, Esq., Author: P. Boyd publisher: Princeton University Press, New Jersey Pgs. 156–159. Accounts, with Legal Records and Miscellany.* August 17, 1774.

85 Ibid.

Other Books by the Author

www.jaynedalessandrocox.com

A Miracle in Bethlehem – A Children's Christmas Story

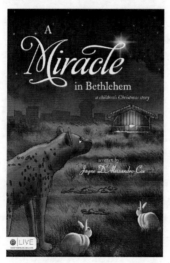

The infant Jesus delights in the young animals that visit Him as He lay in the manger. Tina, one unpopular hyena, experiences the true meaning of Christmas when she comes in contact with the newborn. Her heart is changed forever as the tender field animals watch the transforming experience, under the glowing star of Bethlehem. An audio book download is included in the book. This is a story for children ages ten and under.

To order, visit http://www.tatepublishing.com.

A Passover Blessing

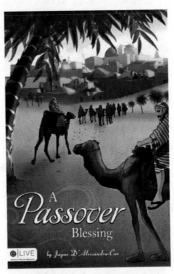

As the 12-year old Jesus speaks in the temple at Passover, a young peasant girl wanders in and is captivated by His teaching. At His feet, Ruth learns the importance of prayer, and the comfort of faith. In response to Jesus' heartfelt prayer, God the Father answers with an unexpected blessing for Ruth. An audio book download is included in the book. This is a story for children ages ten and under.

To order, visit http://www.tatepublishing.com

Happy Birthday Precious Lamb
– A Memoir of Your Birth

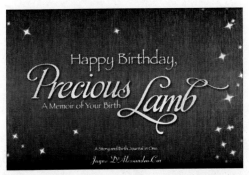

Jesus's mother labors over what special gift she should give her beloved son for His 33rd birthday. Mary lovingly prepares a memoir that documents the circumstances leading up to and surrounding the birth of Jesus, in stunning detail. This very personal journal is now a cherished possession for all generations to read. The book also includes a Baby Journal for new mothers. This is a story for all ages.

To order, visit http://www.tatepublishing.com

Thomas Jefferson statue and author.
Author's personal photo library.
The Colonial Williamsburg Foundation

www.jaynedalessandrocox.com